Technology 2012

Scott Tilley

Precious Publishing
www.PreciousPublishing.biz

ISBN: 1503206009
ISBN-13: 978-1503206007

TABLE OF CONTENTS

DEDICATION

This book is dedicated to everyone at *Florida Today* who helped me with all aspects of publishing a weekly newspaper column throughout 2012. Staying on schedule and meeting deadlines is not always easy, but it's a great way of learning how to write. I can honestly say I've written the Technology Today column on planes, trains, and automobiles – and a few other places as well.

PREFACE

This is a complete collection of my Technology Today columns from 2012. The column appears each week in the business section of the *Florida Today* (Gannett) newspaper. The newspaper primarily serves Brevard County and the Space Coast region of Florida's beautiful east coast.

The columns in this collection are the unedited versions I submit to the newspaper. Sometimes the column in print is shortened to accommodate advertisements or other articles on the page. Any errors or omissions in this book are mine alone.

The newspaper editors craft the headlines for each column; I merely provide a topic or keyword. Sometimes the headline is different in print and online; in these cases I use the print headline as the definitive version. I've included my titles, my suggested catch phrases (sub-titles), and the actual headline used for each column.

The main theme of 2012 was the evolution of computing at the edge (mobile computing), at the center (cloud computing), and in the connections (social computing) of our technical infrastructure. Each of these areas underwent significant changes and dramatic growth. I chose the phrase "To the cloud and beyond" as the book's subtitle to reflect these changes – and because I'm a Buzz Lightyear fan ☺

As always, I hope you find this collection interesting. Please feel free to contact me anytime. I can be reached via email at TechnologyToday@srtilley.com, you can follow my column on Twitter: @TechTodayColumn, and you can find me on Facebook.

Scott Tilley

Melbourne, FL

timeanddate.com

Calendar for year 2012 (United States)

January
S	M	T	W	T	F	S
(1)	(2)	3	4	5	6	7
8	9	10	11	12	13	14
15	(16)	17	18	19	20	21
22	23	24	25	26	27	28
29	30	31				

○:1 ◐:9 ◑:16 ●:23 ◒:30

February
S	M	T	W	T	F	S
			1	2	3	4
5	6	7	8	9	10	11
12	13	14	15	16	17	18
19	(20)	21	22	23	24	25
26	27	28	29			

○:7 ◐:14 ◑:21 ●:29

March
S	M	T	W	T	F	S
				1	2	3
4	5	6	7	8	9	10
11	12	13	14	15	16	17
18	19	20	21	22	23	24
25	26	27	28	29	30	31

○:8 ◐:14 ●:22 ◒:30

April
S	M	T	W	T	F	S
1	2	3	4	5	6	7
8	9	10	11	12	13	14
15	16	17	18	19	20	21
22	23	24	25	26	27	28
29	30					

○:6 ◐:13 ●:21 ◒:29

May
S	M	T	W	T	F	S
		1	2	3	4	5
6	7	8	9	10	11	12
13	14	15	16	17	18	19
20	21	22	23	24	25	26
27	(28)	29	30	31		

○:5 ◐:12 ●:20 ◒:28

June
S	M	T	W	T	F	S
					1	2
3	4	5	6	7	8	9
10	11	12	13	14	15	16
17	18	19	20	21	22	23
24	25	26	27	28	29	30

○:4 ◐:11 ●:19 ◒:26

July
S	M	T	W	T	F	S
1	2	3	(4)	5	6	7
8	9	10	11	12	13	14
15	16	17	18	19	20	21
22	23	24	25	26	27	28
29	30	31				

○:3 ◐:10 ●:19 ◒:26

August
S	M	T	W	T	F	S
			1	2	3	4
5	6	7	8	9	10	11
12	13	14	15	16	17	18
19	20	21	22	23	24	25
26	27	28	29	30	31	

○:1 ◐:9 ●:17 ◒:24 ○:31

September
S	M	T	W	T	F	S
						1
2	(3)	4	5	6	7	8
9	10	11	12	13	14	15
16	17	18	19	20	21	22
23	24	25	26	27	28	29
30						

◐:8 ●:15 ◒:22 ○:29

October
S	M	T	W	T	F	S
	1	2	3	4	5	6
7	(8)	9	10	11	12	13
14	15	16	17	18	19	20
21	22	23	24	25	26	27
28	29	30	31			

◐:8 ●:15 ◒:21 ○:29

November
S	M	T	W	T	F	S
				1	2	3
4	5	6	7	8	9	10
(11)	(12)	13	14	15	16	17
18	19	20	21	(22)	23	24
25	26	27	28	29	30	

◐:6 ●:13 ◒:20 ○:28

December
S	M	T	W	T	F	S
						1
2	3	4	5	6	7	8
9	10	11	12	13	14	15
16	17	18	19	20	21	22
23	24	(25)	26	27	28	29
30	31					

◐:6 ●:13 ◒:20 ○:28

Jan 1	New Year's Day	May 28	Memorial Day	Nov 11	Veterans Day
Jan 2	'New Year's Day' observed	Jun 17	Fathers' Day	Nov 12	'Veterans Day' observed
Jan 16	Martin Luther King Day	Jul 4	Independence Day	Nov 22	Thanksgiving Day
Feb 14	Valentine's Day	Sep 3	Labor Day	Dec 24	Christmas Eve
Feb 20	Presidents' Day	Oct 8	Columbus Day	Dec 25	Christmas Day
Apr 8	Easter Sunday	Oct 31	Halloween	Dec 31	New Year's Eve
May 13	Mothers' Day	Nov 6	Election Day		

x

LOOKING AHEAD TO 2012

Focus on the edge, the center, and the connections of computing

Published as "In 2012, to the cloud and beyond"

January 6, 2012 (456 words)

Technology predictions are notoriously inaccurate, but we make them every year anyway because they're great fun to do. Looking ahead to 2012, I predict that the very nature of what we call "computing" will continue to change. These changes have already begun, but will gain momentum at the edge (mobile computing), in the center (cloud computing), and on the connections (social computing) of our technical infrastructure.

Mobile computing is characterized today by smartphones and tablets, and to a lesser extent, traditional notebook computers. Phones are now the most common type of computer on the planet, and smartphones with apps are fast becoming the de facto computing platform for many people. There's little doubt that this trend towards computing "at the edge" – with tremendous power in peoples' hands when connected to a network – will accelerate in the coming year.

Tablets have created an entirely new market, one they partially share with smartphones. But using a tablet is a different experience than either a smartphone or a notebook. Tablets are very personal devices, useful for reading books, browsing online, and consuming media content. But tablets are having a tremendous impact on the enterprise as well. Many IT groups are struggling to manage important governance issues such as security with new employees who are comfortable with the BYOD ("bring your own device") model of corporate computing.

If smartphones and tablets represent computing at the edge – in the hands of the users – then cloud computing represents computing in the center. This is similar to the old days of mainframe systems, where users connected to large computers via dumb terminals. However, cloud computing is different in part because it offers the possibility of on-demand

1

capabilities. CPU power and data storage can be purchased as a scalable service, reducing the need for expensive in-house setup. As more providers package cloud computing as a low-cost alternative to expensive capital investment, this trend will accelerate in 2012.

The third facet of the computing infrastructure undergoing change is the connectivity between people and between computers. Smartphones and tablets are used at the edge, and cloud computing is in the center. Tying everything together like gossamer threads in the computing ether is social computing, which includes social media like Twitter, supercomputer interfaces like IBM's Watson, and intelligent agents like Apple's Siri.

Most companies now recognize the need to leverage social media. Corporate software is predicted to increasingly resemble websites like Facebook that young employees are familiar with. Crowdsourcing (where a problem is posed to a group of people online) is a powerful way to multiply the knowledge and experience of many individuals. I think this will expand to include computing agents as part of the intelligence network. It will take "googling" to a whole new level

KODAK

They say memories fade but pictures last forever

Published as "Kodak may be fading away"

January 13, 2012 (466 words)

They say memories fade but pictures last forever. Unfortunately, the same can't be said for the company that makes the pictures. Eastman Kodak, an iconic American business for 132 years, may itself soon be fading away.

What caused Kodak's downfall? There were several factors, but arguably the most significant was disruptive digital technology. In many ways, Kodak is following a similar path that brought down Nortel Networks and Borders Books & Music: a failure to quickly adapt to a changing marketplace.

Kodak actually invented the digital camera in 1975, but failed to capitalize on its invention for fear of cannibalizing sales of its lucrative film business. Successful technology companies know that if they don't offer new products – even if these products may hurt the sales of existing products – another company will. For example, Apple did it with the iPhone, which threatened sales of the iPod, and again with the iPad, with threatened sales of the MacBook. Now the iPhone and the iPad together make up more than 50% of Apple's revenue.

Perhaps the problem was that Kodak didn't view itself as a technology company until it was too late; it always viewed itself as an imaging and film company. Kodak was floundering already in 2005 when it made what I think was a disastrous decision to get into the inkjet printer business, which has very low margins in the highly competitive consumer space. He move was driven by CEO Antonio Perez, who joined Kodak from HP in 2005, where he was in charge of their printer business – which is probably why he led Kodak down this path to nowhere.

Kodak had tried to increase its revenue through licensing deals and patent lawsuits, but that's not a strategy for future success. It's living off the past, and in today's technical businesses it never works for very long. The result is that Kodak is down to 19,000 employees, with a share price below $1 (which puts them in danger of being de-listed from the stock exchange), and contemplating a Chapter 11 filing.

Sadly, I believe that Kodak's likely future is indeed bankruptcy. This would be followed by a fire sale of their 1,100 or so patents – the sole remaining asset of value (besides their people) that could raise necessary capital. Bankruptcy would also allow them to get out of their expensive pension and health-care obligations for retirees, which is good news for the company but very bad news for their former employees.

Kodak may emerge from bankruptcy as a competitive – albeit very different – company. Or it may simply disappear, a testament to the dangers of not keeping pace with technical change. Interestingly, sales of camcorders and digital cameras are dropping like a rock: their functions are being replaced by smartphones. Maybe the digital camera boat is already sinking.

SOPA AND PIPA

Not the twins from "Anne of Green Gables"

Published as "SOPA and PIPA? Slippery slopes to avoid"

January 20, 2012 (436 words)

SOPA and PIPA. They sound like two twins from an "Anne of Green Gables" children's story. In reality they are nowhere near as innocent.

SOPA ("Stop Online Piracy Act") is a bill introduced in the House last October. PIPA ("PROTECT IP Act", where PROTECT itself stands for "Preventing Real Online Threats to Economic Creativity and Theft of Intellectual Property") is the Senate's version of the same legislation. SOPA's stated intention is, "To promote prosperity, creativity, entrepreneurship, and innovation by combating the theft of U.S. property, and for other purposes."

Broadly speaking, the big media companies and content creators, like the Motion Picture Association of America (MPAA), are in favor of the bill. They see it as increasing their ability to limit the reach of offshore companies and websites like The Pirate Bay that host or distribute copyrighted material. As a content creator myself, I can see the value in protecting one's intellectual property.

However, newer Internet companies, like Google, are generally against the bill. In fact, this Wednesday, websites like Mozilla and Wikipedia "went dark" to protest SOPA and PIPA. So what are they so concerned about? In a word, lawsuits.

The bills focus on foreign companies, but there is a danger that domestic companies that simply link to them would be liable. For websites that rely on material provided by volunteers, the host and/or the ISP could be held responsible for the content.

An earlier version of the bill would have permitted the US Justice Department to completely block a website based on a single complaint lodged against it. In effect, this would force the ISPs to act as censors on the government's behalf.

To me, this is an egregious overstepping of authority. After all, we complain when other countries like China and Iran block access to certain websites, so why would we want to enable it at home? It's a slippery slope from investigating IP theft to blocking political discussions. It might even prevent the use of proxy servers to support legitimate whistle blowing activity and human rights protests that were so much in the news last year.

I think the Digital Millennium Copyright Act (DMCA) was already too onerous. SOPA will simply force more US-based companies to deal with increasingly burdensome regulations. It's another part of the "full employment act for lawyers," and it's hard to argue that lawyers are a key part of the creative process that drives our knowledge-based economy.

The Senate will vote on PIPA on January 24. I'm certainly not a strident activist, but let's hope that the current virtual strikes have some affect on the thinking in Washington.

How Computing Changed the World

Don't be surprised if something truly amazing happens

Published as "Computers' metamorphoses huge"

January 27, 2012 (454 words)

Few things have changed the modern world as much as computers. A public forum was held last week at the Florida Institute of Technology to discuss the impact of computing on our lives. Phil Chan, a faculty member from the Department of Computer Sciences, moderated the event.

The first speaker was Ronda Henning, a Senior Scientist for Information Assurance at Harris Corporation. She described her own introduction to computing as a choice between pursuing a legal career and accepting a position with the Department of Defense that offered to pay her tuition to study computer science. Many of today's security challenges arise from the increased complexity of the systems that we rely on – and it looks like things will only get more challenging going forward.

The second speaker was Ryan Stansifer, a faculty member from the Department of Computer Sciences at FIT. He described how computing has made it possible to advance our knowledge of basic science and mathematics. Fast Fourier Transforms were used to illustrate how novel algorithms were developed in the 1960s to make image and signal processing practical. This in turn made modern gadgets like digital cameras a reality. Interestingly, the day after the forum, an announcement appeared in the academic press that researchers from MIT had improved the process even further, which shows that there's always room for improvement on solutions to fundamental computing problems.

The third speaker was Rebecca Mazzone, a project manager for NASA with KSC's Information Technology Directorate. She illustrated some of the stark differences in computing power between the processors and storage capacity of the early Apollo moon rockets and today's iPhones. She mentioned the use of advanced artificial intelligence technologies in some of NASA's current robots, including the Mars Rover Opportunity that recently celebrated 8 years on the Red Planet – impressive considering it was supposed to be a 4-month mission.

Following the three presentations there was an open discussion with the audience. I asked the panelists to comment on which areas of our lives computers have **not** made a difference. I offered literature as one example. Ronda felt that classical subjects such as philosophy remained much the same. Ryan commented that education seemed less affected by computing than one would think. Rebecca felt that our "always on" connected society was not necessarily a step in the right direction.

The last topic of the forum was the future of computing. Many panelists felt that health care and medicine would be an area that will see impressive advancements. The advancements will likely be incremental, not revolutionary, due to the complexity of the area. However, no one should be surprised if something truly amazing happens due to improvements in computing that we can't yet imagine. It's happened before.

LOOKIT! LOOKIT! LOOKIT!

Have we become a society of Sallys?

Published as "Social media fans say: 'Lookit me!'"

February 3, 2012 (444 words)

When I was young I used to read "Peanuts" comics all the time. I have a pretty good memory, so many of the images and tag lines have stayed with me through the years. The news of a pending IPO by the social networking giant Facebook reminded me of one strip in particular: Sally is jumping rope and trying to get her brother Charlie Brown to pay attention to her, so she shouts at him, "Lookit! Lookit! Lookit!" Exasperated at being interrupted, he finally replies with a shout of "I'm lookiting!"

Have we become a society of Sallys?

Clearly many people see value in social networks. Wall Street is rumored to place Facebook around $100 billion. It currently has over 800 million users. And each one of them seems to be shouting the same thing: "Lookit! Lookit! Lookit!"

A newer social media platform called Path takes this type of egocentrism to the next level. It limits you to 150 connections. The hook is that this is a more personal social network, so you'll be inclined to share even more personal information with your friends and family online. Is that really a good idea?

Path calls itself a smart journal. I always thought a journal was for personal reflection. It appears that the Path version of a journal is far more exhibitionist. Their advertisement says you use Path to share photos, videos, who you're with, where you are, the music you're listening to, what you're thinking (hah!), when you wakeup and when you go to bed, and when you change location. All this is shared with you in real time.

Does anyone really need to know this sort of minutiae about other people? It's the digital equivalent of Sally shouting "Lookit!" to everyone she knows online. Who cares?

If you've ever been on vacation with other people, you know some folks obsess over taking photos – often to the detriment of enjoying the moment. "I want to show this to so-and-so back home," they'll say. With social networks, why wait? Show them what you're doing while you're doing it. Even if it means ignoring the people you're with in the real world at the time.

I fear social media addicts are becoming like those annoying friends who send glowing holiday letters every Christmas, detailing ad nauseam how their spoiled kids are doing in private school, what fancy holidays they went on, who won what participation award, and so on. The difference now is that we don't have to wait for December; we can receive this stream of blather all the time.

I'm tempted to shout, "I'm lookiting!" just to make it stop, but is anybody listening?

VALENTINE'S DAY

Why I don't work at Hallmark

Published as "Valentine's Day gets a digital boost"

February 10, 2012 (424 words)

How's this for a Valentine's Day poem: "text messages are lazy / e-cards can be crazy / only real cards are good enough for my Daisy"

Yes, well, that's why I don't work at Hallmark. But you understand the sentiment. There is still a place for a real, physical card to send the proper message on February 14. But these days, who has the time to visit the store to pick out a card, go to the Post Office to get the stamps, and drop off the card in the mailbox?

As always, technology comes to the rescue.

There are several smartphone apps now available that let you craft your own personalized greeting card, and then have the card printed and sent by regular mail to that special someone. The fact that they are apps on the phone makes it even more convenient to use, since you can prepare the cards and send them out from anywhere. Just be sure to leave enough time for the Post Office to deliver them.

I've tried a few greeting card apps, but my favorite is Apple's Cards on the iPhone. Like most Apple products, it integrates well with the rest of my programs and data. This means the photos and addresses I have on the phone are synced and available to use when I need them.

I used Cards to send a few Christmas greetings last year. It was a snap to select a layout I liked from the collection of themes Apple provides. You then select any photos you want to appear on the front, inside, and/or back of the card from your own collection. You then enter the personal message you want, again on the front, inside, and/or back, in the font you prefer. If the card's recipient is already in your Address Book, then you can use it automatically; otherwise, you enter the address manually.

The program then shows you a full-color preview of the whole card. If you like how it looks, Cards calculates the postage needed (the cards can be sent to anyone in America for $2.99 and to many international destinations for a few dollars more), your iTunes account is charged the appropriate amount, and Apple takes care of the rest. They print the card, they take care of applying the postage, and they pop it into the mail for you. Easy as pie.

Your Valentine receives a nice, printed card in the mail, complete with glossy photos and personal messages. You look like a thoughtful and caring person. Everyone's happy.

ENGINEERS WEEK

A career as an engineer is a great way to make a difference

Published as "Engineering degrees open myriad job options"

February 17, 2012 (430 words)

Next week is Engineers Week. It's likely you'll hear the phrase "STEM" (Science, Technology, Engineering, and Mathematics) in the news. A career as an engineer is a great way to make a difference: for yourself, for your family, and for our country. To prepare for such a career, it helps to understand the relationship between science, mathematics, technology, and engineering.

Science is the study of basic principles of the world around us. It is a discipline born out of our curiosity to understand how things work at an elemental level. It encompasses areas such as life sciences (e.g., biology and genetics) and physical sciences (e.g., physics and chemistry). A scientist's career involves observation of phenomenon, hypotheses as to why things are the way they seem to be, and repeatable experiments to validate or refute these hypotheses. A scientist's goal is to advance the understanding of the most fundamental aspects of our existence.

Mathematics can be viewed as a form of pure science. It provides the tools needed to formally model and represent aspects of our real world, such as shapes and relationships. It also helps us to logically reason about abstract concepts, such as numbers and time. Some people study pure mathematics as an end in itself. Scientists of all stripes rely on mathematics to help them in their daily tasks, which is why a sound understanding of mathematical principles is so important to their careers.

Technology represents the implementation of tools and techniques to help solve real-world problems. The nature of technology changes over time. For example, the steam engine is a Victorian-era technology that changed the world of transportation. In contrast, a microprocessor represents a much more complex technology developed far more recently.

In both cases, an engineer makes the technology possible in large part through the understanding of basic scientific principles and the application of mathematical formulae.

Engineering is what turns theory into practice. An engineer must master basic science and applied mathematics, but they also need to understand other areas, such as economics and social studies, to have a successful career. As with science, there are different branches of engineering, including classical areas such as civil and mechanical, and newer areas such as aerospace and software.

If you're a student, becoming an engineer means you'll be able to choose between exciting careers, doing amazing things such as designing the world's tallest skyscraper, developing the next-generation of quantum computers, or founding the next Facebook. If you're a parent or an educator, encourage your charges to follow a career in engineering. They'll be in for a wild ride.

CLOUD SECURITY

What should we be concerned about?

Published as "Cloud computing lifts security bar"

February 24, 2012 (432 words)

Cloud computing is hot. But what are cooling down some people's enthusiasm for it are the security risks (perceived or real).

Is cloud security something that we need to be concerned about?

Do get an answer to this question, I spoke with Fred Hawkes, an Information Security Systems Engineer at Harris Corp. He recently obtained the Certificate of Cloud Security Knowledge (CCSK) issued by the Cloud Security Alliance. Fred shared his views of cloud security and the role of certification at a recent meeting of the Space Coast Chapter of the Information Systems Security Association (ISSA) at Florida Tech.

Technology Today: What is the most important "new" thing about cloud computing that industry professionals need to know?

Fred Hawkes: Governance, management, security, and technology are still evolving. Industry professionals need to understand the dynamics and the risks involved before making large commitments in cloud computing.

Technology Today: What are the top three security issues that organizations should be aware of, if they are considering migrating to the cloud?

Fred Hawkes: These would include the uncertainty of achieving and maintaining compliance to governmental regulations (e.g., HIPAA), potential loss of control of an organization's governance structure, and the additional risks that accompany the sharing of resources with other companies, including the service provider.

Technology Today: What sort of organization is not suited to the cloud?

Fred Hawkes: Organizations that have highly sensitive data, clients, and applications that cannot or should not be exposed to the additional risks associated with cloud computing either in a public or private (internal environment) until such time as the organization can assure the preservation of the confidentiality and integrity of the assets they must protect.

Technology Today: Will getting CSSK certification help someone find a job?

Fred Hawkes: For the next year or so, I think it will only help those looking for work with an organization preparing to move into the cloud computing arena. Having the certificate means that you have a well-rounded knowledge of cloud computing, its risks and challenges. Through this knowledge, you can provide support to organizational decision makers actively investigating cloud computing.

Technology Today: How does this certificate differ from other security certificates?

Fred Hawkes: The CCSK differs from the CISSP primarily in that it has several additional "domains of knowledge" above that of the CISSP that focus on virtual computing technology, management of the supply chain, and interoperability and portability between cloud suppliers.

Technology Today: Where do you see cloud computing in five years?

Fred Hawkes: Cloud computing will be another entrenched computing paradigm that IT organizations will include in their operating environment.

LEAP YEAR

2000 was a Leap Year, so why wasn't 1900?

Published as "Leap Year calculation not so clear cut"

March 2, 2012 (432 words)

This year is a Leap Year. Those who are fortune enough to be born on Leap Day (February 29) enjoy permanent youth due to the vagaries of our calendar, since their birthday only occurs every four years.

Determining whether or not a year is a leap year is not quite as simple as most people think. In fact, I often use this calculation as a programming exercise for my students. Most people assume that every year divisible by 4, such as 2008, is a leap year – but that's not strictly true. If a year is evenly divisible by 100, it is not a leap year unless it is also evenly divisible by 400. For example, 2000 was a leap year, but 1900 was not.

We have leap years because the earth does not revolve around the sun in exactly 365 days: it's more like 365 days and 6 hours. So every 4 years we add an extra day to the Gregorian calendar. Actually, it's a bit less than 6 hours, which is why we make further adjustments every 400 years.

It would be nice is such adjustments were not needed, but nature doesn't always follow nice, round numbers. In fact, the very notion of time and dates on a calendar are artificial means for us to track the passage of events. Have you ever wondered how the length of a second was decided?

Not too long ago, we had sundials that used solar shadows to track the progress of a day. It is difficult to measure individual minutes with a sundial (assuming the sun is out), never mind individual seconds. A few hundred years ago we switched to mechanical clocks, which use springs and wheels to measure time. About 30 years ago digital clocks became popular; they use the oscillations of a tiny crystal to measure time more accurately.

The gold standard today for measuring time are atomic clocks. Since 1967, the official definition of a second has been the time needed for

9,192,631,770 cycles of a Cesium 133 atom to switch between two energy states. It's actually even more precise than that: the atoms must be measured at sea level, to accommodate minor discrepancies due to relativity. These clocks are so accurate that they will lose less than one second in 100 million years.

It might be nice to return to a simple circadian rhythm: get up with the sun and go to bed shortly after nightfall. But our modern lives are obsessed with time. Just count the number of clocks in your house, in your car, and in your gadgets.

CUTTING THE CABLE

The traditional broadcast model for TV is broken

Published as "Added cable fees too much for him"

March 9, 2012 (447 words)

In the end it was the additional $9.95 per month that broke the camel's back.

Like many people, I was on a promotional package for several months from my local cable company. But then the promotion ended and my costs went up by $9.95. When I called and asked if the price could be reduced, the answer was a clear "no" – the lower price was for new customers only. I've often wondered why companies are willing to let new customers pay less than their existing customers. Well, if the company wasn't going to be loyal to me, I felt no need to be loyal to them.

I took a look at my itemized costs on the most recent monthly bill. In addition to the increase of $9.95 that was part of a packaged bundle of digital cable and Internet access, I was paying an extra $15 for "turbo" network access and an additional $9.95 for HD DVR rental. That amounts to $35 per month that I could no longer justify.

I called the cable company back and told them I was dumping my DVR. And the digital cable. And the turbo speed. They didn't even try to keep me as a so-called "premium" customer.

I don't really miss the increased Internet speed because I rarely experienced it in daily use. I had bursts of speed, but not sustained speeds. There are many other issues that can cause common activities like accessing a website to be slow, such as buggy DNS (domain name server) resolution – which unfortunately I had a lot.

My complex already provides basic digital cable, including several HD channels. The reality is that I almost never watch live TV anymore; I can't stand the commercials (which is why I used the DVR). Out of 30 minutes, most shows run about 18 minutes of content (plus the opening and closing credits); the rest are ads. I'd pay a modest fee to watch the few shows I like without commercials – and in fact I do, just not through the cable company.

So now I've cut the cord. I have basic digital cable, but only because it's provided. I watch streaming content via Netflix, Amazon.com, and Apple on my TV. I watch other content on my computer.

The only reason I still have any interaction with the cable company is that they are the sole source of Internet access in my area. But that will change.

It's very obvious that the traditional broadcast model for TV is broken. Sooner or later, the cable companies will go the way of Blockbuster: out of business. Internet access will become a utility, like water or electricity, and I'll use it accordingly.

GOODBYE CRUEL PHYSICAL WORLD

Our world is becoming increasingly digital

Published as "Newest transistors get still tinier"

March 16, 2012 (426 words)

There's a saying in computer science that the only thing real is the source code. And even that's not "real" in the physical sense; it's more like ephemeral words on a page.

Two developments this week emphasized how our world is becoming increasingly digital. The first is that scientists have created a single-atom transistor. The second is that Encyclopedia Britannica is ending publication of its printed edition. For many analog technologies, it's "Goodbye, cruel physical world."

Single-Atom Transistors: I first became interested in electronics by doing TV repair. At the time, televisions still commonly used vacuum tubes. I was fascinated by how they worked. Tubes were more sophisticated than simple relays, but they were still physical items that you could touch and hold. The cathode glowed with a reassuring warmth to indicate the tube was on and (probably) working.

When transistors began to replace vacuum tubes, something tactile was lost. I had to use test equipment to find out if a transistor was working or not; there is no way to tell just by looking at it (unless it melted or blew up in spectacular fashion). As transistors were packed by the hundreds then thousands and now millions onto integrated circuits, their inner workings became more of a black box. Something magic was going on in there, but it was hard to understand exactly what or how.

Now comes news that transistors have been created using a single phosphorous atom. This means that one day it will be possible to pack billions of transistors onto a single chip smaller than your thumbnail. They will be faster, use less energy, and be more powerful than anything we have today. But you won't be able to hold one, or really see what's going on in these tiny devices without equally advanced tools such as scanning tunneling microscopes – a long way from just eyeballing the circuit board.

Encyclopedia Britannica Online: Stop the press. Literally. The venerable Encyclopedia Britannica is going online only. After more than 200 years of publishing the definitive guide to human knowledge in book form, soon you will only be able to access this content in digital format.

I have to admit that I never owned a copy of the entire encyclopedia, but that's mostly due to cost: the retail price for the hardcover edition is currently $1,395. I did use it though, mostly at the library or at work. There was something reassuring about holding the heavy volumes, flipping through its pages and reading articles of interest.

Now most people use Google and WikiPedia instead.

THE THREE PS

Programming, presenting, and publishing

Published as "Tech career? Master the Three Ps"

March 23, 2012 (427 words)

We're all familiar with the "three Rs" of elementary school: reading, writing and arithmetic. All children are encouraged to master these skills as part of their basic education. To be successful in technology today, you also need to master the "three Ps": **p**rogramming, **p**resenting, and **p**ublishing.

When most people think of a career in technology they think of computers, and programming is a very important part of computing. Without software programs – and the people to write them – computers would be little more than expensive paperweights. It is for this reason that so much of an undergraduate computer science student's time is spent learning various programming languages and associated tools.

However, just as knowing how to spell doesn't make you a great author, knowing how to program doesn't make you a great engineer. You may be an excellent programmer, but if you can't explain your work to your peers then your career will quickly plateau. This means the most important language you should master is not C# or Java – it's English.

You need proficiency in English to present and publish your work. These are two communication skills that have become absolutely essential to success. As the complexity of modern technology increases, so does the importance of being able to explain complex concepts to your colleagues and customers in a way that they can easily understand.

Many people have a fear of public speaking. Fortunately there are organizations such as Toast Masters that can help you overcome these fears. You don't need to become Tony Robbins; all you need is to become comfortable and adept at presentations. As you move up the career ladder, having a combination of deep technical knowledge and excellent verbal communication skills are one of the ways to stand out from the crowd.

Similarly, publishing your work in written form is fundamental skill that you should master. Whether it's contributing to a company blog, writing white papers and reports, or writing a substantial document like a book, it's all writing. As with speaking skills, writing skills can be learned over time. All you need to do is take the time to practice and hone your skills.

For each of the three Ps there is technology that can help. For example, for programming there are sophisticated development environments. For presenting there are lots of examples of how to organize your thoughts and speak to an audience – even if it's recorded and not live the first few times (e.g., via YouTube). For publishing there are many tools that can help with outlining, grammar, sentence structure, and copyediting.

SOFTWARE TESTING

Ghosts in the machine

Published as "Software testers serve crucial role"

March 30, 2012 (434 words)

If the Ghostbusters had a software division, you'd know whom to call when your computer crashed. After all, it often seems like there are ghosts in the machine. How else can you explain why programs don't do what you expect them to do?

Luckily, the reasons programs don't always work as planned rarely include the paranormal. Just like an old "Scooby Doo" episode, where the ghost turns out to be a regular criminal, the reasons programs fail are usually more mundane. But instead of Shaggy, Daphne, and the gang, we rely on software testers to help us catch the culprits.

A primary goal of a software tester is to find bugs in programs. A "bug" is some part of the program that is not working properly. The word "bug" actually harkens back to a simpler time in computing, when a literal bug – a moth – was stuck between the contact plates of a relay of an early computer, causing it to malfunction.

Today's software is so large, complex, and important that it's essential that testing be performed professionally and effectively. Special forms of testing, such as security testing, are particularly critical. A recent statement from a retiring FBI executive saying our current efforts to combat cyber attacks are insufficient speaks to the importance of this type of software testing for our national infrastructure.

Without proper software testing, bad things can happen – things that can affect every our daily lives. For example, many of the transactions made on the stock exchange are done using automated trading systems that buy and sell shares many times a second – far faster than a human trader. One such system malfunctioned in February 2010, causing oil futures to fluctuate wildly. According to *The Economist*, the cause was eventually determined to be a new program that had been turned on the day before, but that was only tested for one hour. The usual testing period for these programs is six to eight weeks. Bugs in the code went undetected until the program malfunctioned, causing hundreds of thousands of dollars of losses and fines.

There are many hard problems in software testing. Some are people issues (e.g., education and training), some are process issues (e.g., how testing is conducted within an organization), and some are technology issues (e.g., which tools are used). What is clear is that the skills needed by a good software tester are increasingly broad and deep.

Fortunately, software testing is an attractive career. A recent article in *Forbes* magazine ranked software testing as "the happiest job in the US." With a typical salary of $85,000, who can blame them?

SWAMPED

Florida's natural state

Published as "Shouldn't technology simplify things?"

April 6, 2012 (440 words)

There's a word that keeps appearing with alarming frequency in recent communications with colleagues from around the world: "swamped." They're not referring to our natural Florida habitat. They're referring to being too busy.

The word usually appears in sentences like, "Sorry for the delay in replying. I've been swamped."

I thought technology was supposed to lighten our workload. Remember all those promises of the paperless office? I must have missed the memo, because it doesn't seem to be true for me at all.

There's an old saying that if you want something done, give it do a busy person. This may seem counter-intuitive, but the thinking is that if someone is busy, they're probably quite efficient at managing multiple tasks, and therefore doing "one more thing" is something they can handle. But everyone has their breaking point, and I think for many people these days, they've hit that limit.

I firmly believe that one of the reasons we're so swamped is that we're multi-tasking to the point of inefficiency. In computer science there's a similar phenomenon with operating systems, called "thrashing", where the computer is switching so rapidly between tasks that it doesn't have enough time to spend on any one of them before it moves to the next one.

I believe that we're thrashing in our jobs. Just think of how you spend your own time at work. How many windows are open on your computer screen? How often do you check your email? Facebook updates? Twitter feeds? Text messages on your smartphone?

Our "always on" lives don't help either. Being connected to the office and to friends 24/7 can be useful, but it can also be a colossal waste of time and energy. We rarely get the chance to focus on one thing at a time.

It's like we've all volunteered to have ADD.

I sometimes use a word processor called OmniWriter that is specifically designed to focus your attention on one task: writing. Not formatting. Not playing with fonts. Just typing words onto a page. The program takes over your whole screen with a tranquil image of a calm winter setting in a forest; relaxing soft music plays in the background. When you work in such an environment you start to realize how distracted we are most of the time.

Paradoxically, there are many programs that you can use to track your time, but you need to learn how to use them first, and who has time for that? Personally I'm going to try to learn how to manage my time a bit better in the future. But first I just have to check my email …

FLAME BOY

In cyberspace, everyone can hear you scream

Published as "Not a jerk? Then don't be one online"

April 13, 2012 (428 words)

There is a famous tag line from the movie Alien: "In space, no one can hear you scream." When people are online, there is a certain sense of anonymity, so maybe we need a new tagline: "In cyberspace, everyone can hear you scream." But of course most people aren't listening to you anyway.

Moreover, the sense of anonymity people feel when they are online is misplaced. You can try to hide behind pseudonyms, obscure user names, and spoofed Internet addresses, but if someone wants to find you, they will. Law enforcement does it all the time.

The false sense of anonymity can turn a polite Dr. Jekyll into an obnoxious Mr. Hyde when online. People write things in forums and chat rooms that they would never say to your face. It's very odd that basic manners seem to disappear so quickly.

Of course, similar things happen in the real world as well. We've all experienced enraged drivers angrily shaking their fists at us for the most minor perceived offense. The closed windows and the apparent safety of being in another car that can quickly drive away from the confrontation provides the distance needed to separate polite discussion from vulgar swearing.

The problem is exacerbated in cyberspace because there is always distance between people. Sometimes that distance is time – for example, between posting a comment and reading a reply later. Sometimes it's the lack of physical closeness – and therefore no imminent fear of an actual altercation.

There's even a word given to people who act like this online: "Flame Boy", which I first read in a Dilbert cartoon in 1995. In the strip, Dilbert writes that Wally's, "ignorance seems to have no limits … [his] opinions are idiotic." Dilbert then further baits Wally by writing in his email, "Your personal hygiene leaves much to be desired." Wally peers over the cubicle wall and says to Dilbert, "You're mighty brave in cyberspace, Flame Boy."

I consider this sort of action to be unacceptable. Like many people, I have learned to mostly ignore online rants and vile comments. But I'd prefer that people realize that there are ethical rules of behavior in cyberspace just like there are ethical codes of conduct in our regular society.

There's a simple rule of thumb that can be followed to maintain your status as a good cyber-citizen. Would you say in person, face to face, what you write online? If not, don't do it. Remember, once it's online, it never goes away. The old saying, "What goes around, comes around," is even truer in cyberspace.

DISCOVERY

Local hero flies away into the sunrise

Published as "Can victory lap inspire giant leap?"

April 20, 2012 (429 words)

I watched Discovery fly off into the sunrise on Tuesday. I thought I was going to feel sad, knowing that this was the very last time I'd ever see the orbiter in the air. Although I did feel a bit melancholy at this bittersweet event, for the first time in quite a while I also felt optimistic about the future of the space program.

Here in Florida on the Space Coast we're spoiled in many ways, not the least of which was the regular opportunity to see shuttles take off and land in our own backyard. Everyone who has experienced a nighttime launch will tell you how spectacular it is to see and to hear. We've all felt our house shake with the twin sonic booms heralding the shuttle's return. And occasionally we've seen the shuttle being majestically ferried home on the back of a modified 747 jumbo jet.

But the people in DC have never seen any of these things (unless they were lucky enough to visit our beautiful beaches). For the politicians and policy makers in the nation's capitol, seeing Discovery's low-altitude fly-by first hand (not just on TV) should have been inspiring. Discovery is a symbol of American technical know-how, but it's also a symbol of hope. Seeing it silhouetted against the sky with the Mall and the Jefferson Memorial in the frame succinctly captures what is possible when we work together towards a grand goal. Hopefully, such images will personalize the space program for the folks in DC – and when it's personal, they might care about it a little more.

Maybe it will make them think of Discovery's wonderful achievements, from its first launch on Aug. 30, 1984 to its final launch on Feb. 24, 2011. In 27 years of active service it had 39 successful missions. It flew over 149 million miles. It spent over a year (366 days) in space. It was the first shuttle to fly after both the Challenger and Columbia accidents. In more ways than one, Discovery led the way.

The shuttle program, like the Apollo program before it, inspired generations of youngsters to follow a career in science, technology, engineering, or mathematics. As I wrote here almost a year ago, it certainly inspired me. What is needed now is a clear agenda for our next small steps towards the stars.

In the old westerns, and the end of the movie the hero rides away into the sunset. This week, our local hero flew away into the sunrise. I'll take that as a sign of a beginning, not an ending.

TECHNOLOGY FOR THE ARTS

There's an app for that

Published as "Apps just a tool to explore your inner artist"

April 27, 2012 (14 words)

This weekend is the Melbourne Art Festival. It's a wonderful opportunity to experience some of the impressive efforts of Florida artists. It should also inspire you to explore your own inner artist.

What's that? Like the proverbial wannabe singer who can't carry a tune in a suitcase, you think you lack the necessary skills to be an artist? Not so! As with most things these days, technology can help. In fact, there's an app for that.

If you like to take photos, but would like to make them look more attractive and professional, consider Instagram. This is a free app for the iPhone and Android that is hugely popular. It lets you apply numerous special effects and filters to your photos and share the results with your friends on social networks. Facebook was so impressed with the app that they bought Instagram a few weeks ago for $1 billion.

If you prefer drawing, there is a free app called Draw Something for the iPhone and Android that mixes gaming, social networks, and drawing. Think Pictionary but on your phone. The gaming aspect makes you forget that your learning by example from others how to draw. The results can be very funny – and very inspiring.

If you're more of a visual and tactile person, take a look at Pinterest. There's a free iPhone app but many people use the website directly. It lets you create a virtual pinboard that can hold anything: images, video, or text. If you like scrapbooking, you'll like Pinterest. You can design online collages for school assignments. You can plan events like weddings. You can even showcase your favorite hobby.

Technology can't replace the need to understand and master the fundamental artistic skills required to excel in a particular medium. Just like a word processor doesn't make you a good writer, a smartphone app doesn't make you a good painter. Fortunately, there's another set of apps that can help you learn the fundamentals. For example, Mahalo.com offers a free app called Learn to Draw that walks you through the basics of drawing using video lessons on your smartphone. There are similar lessons for other artistic forms, such as sculpture, jewelry, and digital media.

Artists have always used tools to support their creative activities. Apps are just the latest in a long line of developments, from the horsehair paintbrush to video compositors. Hopefully the app technology piques your interest enough to lead you into the rich and rewarding world of the arts.

JAVA APPLETS

I choose to stay disabled

Published as "Tech failures can cost a company"

May 4, 2012 (435 words)

Last night I wasted nearly an hour trying to buy tickets online to an upcoming concert. They say a fool and his money are soon parted. But with technology today, sometimes you just can't get companies to take your money, no matter how hard you try – or how foolish you are.

The problem was a Java applet that the website was using to let you select the seats you want in the concert hall. Java applets are small programs that run within a web browser. They are also the source of numerous problems.

Over a decade ago, Java applets were seen as a savior of the thin-client computing movement. Who needs to install expensive software programs on your PC when you can access everything with just a browser and an Internet connection? Sun Microsystems designed the Java programming language to run in all browsers without change, but the reality was more like, "write once, debug everywhere." Oracle now controls Java, but the situation hasn't improved very much.

Microsoft created their own technology, called ActiveX controls, to run programs in their Internet Explorer browser. The controls worked (sometimes), but they posed a huge security risk, since they gave the applet total access to your computer. ActiveX controls have since been discontinued.

Using Apple's Safari browser, the Java applet from the concert hall refused to load. There was no error message, just a blank screen. I eventually tracked the problem down to a recent security patch that Apple issued for Java.

I next tried the Mozilla Firefox browser. This time I received an error message – sort of. There was a bit of text that I had to scroll down to find, which said, "Inactive Plug-in." When I clicked on the tiny arrow, a window popped up that said, "To use this applet from 'sa1.seatadvisor.com,' you need to enable the Java plug-in. You need to restart your browser after enabling." I chose to stay disabled.

I decided to try Google's Chrome browser. This time the Java applet did load and display the seating chart … and then it hung. The computer displayed the dreaded "beach ball," which is the Mac equivalent of the PC's hourglass, which means the system is stuck. Eventually I got an error message that said, "Aw, Snap! Something went wrong while displaying this webpage. To continue, reload or go to another page."

At least the Google developers had a sense of humor. I decided to follow their advice: I went to another page. I didn't buy the tickets, and the company lost my business. All because of a poorly designed and poorly engineered website

HEXBUGS

Impressive technology masquerading as a toy

Published as "Hexbugs: creepy-crawlies with a robotic touch"

May 11, 2012 (450 words)

When I was a young boy I used to collect bugs from the nearby field. I kept them in glass jars. Looking back, I know this was a cruel thing to do, but creepy-crawlies are part of many boys' childhoods, and I was no different.

I was fascinated with how Daddy Long-Legs spiders moved their eight spindly legs. I swear the Praying Mantis seemed to look right at you with its emerald-colored triangular head and alien eyes.

I'm most certainly not a young boy anymore, but some of the basic interests never really go away. That's why I was so pleasantly surprised to discover a new type of bug this week: a robotic one.

For once, I don't mean a "software bug," which is an error in a program. I mean a real piece of hardware, a "digital bug" that you can hold in your hand. That is, as long as you're not squeamish.

It's called the Hexbug, from Innovation First Labs Inc., and it is impressive piece of technology masquerading as a toy. The least expensive model, called the Nano, costs just $5.99 at local stores. The Nano looks like an integrated circuit, about 2" long, except the pins are its feet, and when they vibrate the bug scuttles across the floor in a very realistic – even vaguely disconcerting – manner. It turns around when it hits an object like the wall. It can even flip itself back on its feet if it gets turned over. It most closely resembles a robotic cockroach, which can be a little unnerving when you see it moving.

There are other Hexbugs, such as crabs, spiders, ants, inchworms, and larvae. The larva model has an infrared sensor near its nose, so it veers away from objects before it touches them. The sight of a slithering robotic bug that looks like a giant slug is not for the faint of heart.

I find the crab model the most disturbing. It sits quietly in a dark corner, and then scuttles around when it senses light or hears noise, before settling down again. All that's missing are the red glowing Terminator-like eyes to give it a full-on freaky effect.

If you are familiar with the TV show "Stargate Atlantis: SG-1," then you may remember the intelligent robots called Replicators. The original Hexbug looks a lot like them: unnatural and unsettling but intriguing.

In some ways, robotic bugs are even better than the real thing. For example, they don't die from lack of oxygen or lack of food. However, they do die when their battery runs out.

Hexbugs are educational and great fun to play with – even for professors like me who are still young boys at heart.

FCAT

The negative role of technology in writing

Published as "FCAT fiasco more proof literacy's dying"

May 18, 2012 (406 words)

When I read that only about a third of students passed the writing portion of the FCAT this year, I wasn't too surprised. But I was surprised that one of the reasons given for the poor results was from, "…increasing emphasis on such conventions as spelling, punctuation and capitalization."

Since when are spelling, punctuation, and capitalization merely "conventions"?

Call me old fashioned, but I still think spelling, punctuation, and grammar are important parts of writing.

In this column, I recently wrote how important it is for engineering graduates to learn how to communicate in English. The recent FCAT results indicate that the problem goes much deeper. Lowering the passing grade to 50% might solve this year's fiasco, but it certainly doesn't address the fundamental problem of literacy for our students.

```
fcat flunk lol

wht u xpct 404

wrtng rus wsic
```

Technology does have a role to play here – a negative role. The shorthand used for instant messages is permeating communications. I often have students send me email using the language they use to send texts to their friends. I'm their professor, not their bff.

Spell checkers have become a crutch that we all rely on. The ubiquitous red line under our typed words has become the norm rather than the exception. When Word is not used, the squiggles disappear – and so does the auto-correct.

Cursive handwriting is also going the way of the dodo. Several states are dropping penmanship instruction from their curricula, opting instead for, "basic typing skills." This would be funny if it wasn't so wrong in so many ways. Keyboards are a technology of the past, not of the future.

I believe there is a more fundamental transformation taking place: writing as we know it is changing. In many ways, we're going backwards. We're regressing from elegant prose to finger-painting.

People used to write books and articles that went through some form of external review. Blogs soon emerged to democratize the publishing process. The popularity of Twitter further abridged communication to 140 characters, complete with a new shorthand language. Now even Twitter is being eclipsed by photo services like Instagram and visually oriented websites like Pinterest. Why tweet when you can just snap a photo or post a picture?

Ancient civilizations used pictograms and hieroglyphics to communicate. Perhaps this is a more natural way to "speak" to one another. If so, the next version of Word will surely have a stick-figure input mode.

NUCLEAR GREEN EGGS AND HAM

You can't get much spicier than radioactive

Published as "Theoretically green eggs, hold the ham"

May 25, 2012 (421 words)

I have a certain glow about me today. Not the sort of glow that makes a pregnant woman look happy and content. More the sort of glow caused by ingesting radioactive isotopes. A Chernobyl type of glow – but in a good way.

My breakfast came straight from the kitchen of Dr. Seuss: nuclear green eggs and ham. Although I don't think Sam I Am's dish was nuclear. And, alas, there was no ham. But the eggs I ate (which were yellow, not green) were good. Fortunately, my tastes lean towards the spicy, and the eggs were flavored with technetium-99m (Tc-99m), a radioisotope commonly used in nuclear medicine procedures. You can't get much spicier than radioactive.

Nuclear medicine is a unique combination of science, medicine, and technology. It involves the beneficial use of radioactive material to diagnose (and sometimes treat) diseases, notably various forms of cancer. Radiation therapy can be traced back a hundred years to the pioneering work of Marie Curie.

Technetium (Tc) is a shiny metal, rarely found in nature. Nearly all of it used in nuclear medicine is artificially manufactured. Tc-99m is an isomer of Tc-99.

The Tc-99m in my eggs began its half-life in a nuclear reactor in Chalk River, Canada. (Why we don't produce it here is a mystery to me.) It was produced during the fission of uranium 235, which creates molybdenum-99 (Mo-99). The Mo-99 atoms decay into Tc-99m, which you then ingest. The Tc-99m eventually decays into Tc-99, which is essentially inert.

When the Tc-99m moves through your body and slowly decays, it releases gamma rays, which are detected by special cameras. Think of the visible trace left across the sky from a nighttime rocket launch, which we can see with the naked eye. In nuclear medicine, the eggs are the rocket, and the trace is not orange flame but the invisible gamma rays.

In my case, the detector was attached to a huge donut-shaped contraption built by Siemens. Unlike an MRI, which produces a terrible clanging racket when used, the Siemens medical imaging machine was mercifully silent. I passed the time listening to a podcast (about technology, naturally) on my iPhone.

When one hears the word "nuclear," many people immediately think of polluting reactors and atomic bombs. Yet for millions of patients, nuclear medicine represents the difference between life and death. Like all treatments and prescriptions, using nuclear material on a human body can have negative side effects. But overall I think the benefits outweigh the risks. But then again, I like life spicy.

SUMMER READING

Three technology-related books I heartily recommend

Published as "Light summer reading: Relativity, cybersecurity, algorithms. Really. "

June 1, 2012 (408 words)

Memorial Day has come and gone, which means summer is officially here. (Never mind what the calendar says.) Summer is traditionally a time to select a few good books for leisurely reading. Here are three technology-related books that I heartily recommend.

The first book is "Schneier on Security" by Bruce Schneier (Wiley, 2008). Schneier has true research credentials, having authored the best-selling textbook "Applied Cryptography" in 1995. I devoured one of his later books, "Secrets and Lies: Digital Security in a Networked World" (Wiley, 2000), in just a few days while at the beach. Schneier's writing is very accessible and easy to follow – which is particularly important given the complex subject of cyber-security that he primarily writes about. If you're interested in reading a collection of essays from an acknowledged leader in a field that permeates our modern lives, then "Schneier on Security" is the book for you.

If your interest runs more towards understanding how computers work at a fundamental level, then the book "9 Algorithms that Changed the Future" by John MacCormick (Princeton University Press, 2012) is a good choice. Algorithms are the heart of computer science; they are the recipes for how to solve a problem. The topic may sound rather dry, but algorithms affect your life every day. For example, every time you search on Google you are relying on the "PageRank" algorithm that underlies the technology used to automatically find what your looking for on the web. We also rely on data compression algorithms to store our digital photos and videos, to stream movies online, and even to watch cable TV. MacCormick does an excellent job of making these academic topics understandable.

Underlying computing is mathematics, and central to mathematics are equations. If you've ever wondered what E=mc2 *really* means, the book "In Pursuit of the Unknown: 17 Equations that Changed the World" by Ian Stewart (Basic Books, 2012) does an admirable job of explaining it. I remember wondering what derivatives and integrals really meant in the physical world when I first studied calculus. It was only later that the notions of acceleration and area under a curve were explained to me. It would have helped me a lot if I had a book like this one to provide the backstory to Newton's work. As for Einstein's famous equation, it is the epitome of elegance, and reading about how it was discovered adds a wonderful sense of adventure to the magic of relativity.

THUMBS UP, THUMBS DOWN

Judging technology's winners and losers in the news

Published as "Technology winners, losers in the news"

June 8, 2012 (421 words)

There's been so much technology news lately that I thought I'd borrow the newspaper's comment mechanism and give my opinion on some of the recent developments. We've certainly been living up to our area's namesake of the Space Coast. It's all space, all the time!

Thumbs up: To SpaceX, for re-igniting interest the space program. I was at the river's edge in the wee hours of the morning for the first launch attempt, and was there again a few days later to see the Falcon 9 blast off from Cape Canaveral into the night sky. I watched the Dragon capsule dock with the ISS on NASA TV. When the capsule successfully splashed down into the Pacific last Thursday, it marked a positive turning point for the privatization of space.

Thumbs down: To Facebook, for plans to lure adolescents and children under 13 onto its social networking website. Under the new proposal, kids would create accounts under parental supervision, with the parent's account linked to their kids' accounts. I see this primarily as a calculated way for Facebook to grow its user base ahead of privacy regulations and indoctrinate increasingly young users into social media.

Thumbs up: To the International Space University (ISU). The 25th ISU Space Studies Program is being held this summer at Florida Tech and KSC. The 130+ young scientists and engineers (plus faculty) from over 30 countries are each a positive reminder that the future of space is in good hands.

Thumbs up and down: To the federal government for admitting that it was behind the Stuxnet virus that attacked Iran's nuclear facilities. News reports stated that the US geek squad, working with the Israelis – and maybe others – engineered the crafty virus. The good news is that the virus worked: it slowed down the development of weapons-grade uranium. The bad news is that like all weapons, Stuxnet can be turned against us. The more recent Flame malware is even more sophisticated, and once in the wild it becomes more difficult to control – or to counter, if it was altered to attack our own infrastructure. Cyberwarfare is a dangerous and unpredictable business.

Thumbs up: To the local institutions like Florida Tech and BCC for making the transition of Venus a teachable – and an enjoyable – moment for everyone. Cloudy weather made it hard to see Venus, but there's an app for that! Learning how trigonometry was used hundreds of years ago to estimate the distance from the Earth to the Sun was fascinating. We won't see this again until 2117.

FATHER'S DAY

Remote-control software for your computer

Published as "Help Dad demystify his PC from afar"

June 15, 2012 (449 words)

Most holidays are at the same time every year, yet they still seem to appear on the horizon like an unforeseen event. Father's Day is no different. If you're still struggling with gift ideas for what to give dear old dad, save yourself a lot of time and aggravation with remote control software for his computer.

If you're of a certain age, it's highly likely that your father grew up in a very different technological era. In particular, he probably spent much of his working life without the need for a computer on his desk. It's only in retirement that he's experienced the joys and the frustrations of the modern PC.

Those of us who know technology, who understand how computers work (both hardware and software), sometimes forget all the implicit knowledge we use when dealing with PCs. It's a common mistake to assume that everyone else has the same background. If you've ever spent hours on the telephone with someone trying to fix a problem with their computer, without really seeing their screen, and relying solely on their floundering description of what's going on, then you know how challenging it can be.

Remote control software solves this problem. A small program is installed on your dad's computer (which must be connected to the Internet). You run another program on your own computer (Mac or Windows), which can be thousands of miles away from his. The two programs talk to one another securely across the network. The result is that you see everything on dad's computer screen on your computer screen – in real time. Even better, you can control his mouse and type into his computer just like you were sitting beside him. In effect, his remote computer becomes your local computer.

There are several programs that let you perform this magic. Microsoft offers Remote Desktop Connection, but it requires a special server version of Windows running on dad's machine (which is not common). A very popular commercial program called GoToMyPC from Citrix is available for about $10/month. If you need to control more than one computer, say dad's PC in one city and a friend's PC in another city, you can buy more advanced plans.

I've used a free program called LogMeIn for many years now, and it's done the job for me. It lets you view the remote PC in a browser window. There's even versions for the iPad and iPhone if you need to make a quick fix while on the road.

Remote control software will save your dad from tedious and confusing chores, like running Windows update, so that he can just use his computer. And believe me, remote control software will save you too.

Retina Displays

It's all fun and games until someone looses an eye

Published as "Enhanced display is the Apple of his eye"

June 22, 2012 (423 words)

Ever since the iPhone 4 came out, I've been wondering how Apple used tiny eyeballs in their displays. I know they're eyeballs, because the screen is called a "retina display" – and a retina is part of an eye. I know they're tiny, because I can't see any of them. Well, not with my own big eyes, anyway.

To find out how Apple accomplished this amazing feat of bioengineering, I did some research into retina displays. Imagine my surprise to discover that the displays aren't actually made of tiny eyeballs at all! Serves me right for trusting Wikipedia.

Retina displays are essentially the same as all other computer displays. They are made of glass and liquid crystals forming millions of tiny pixels ("picture elements") that glow to produce the image you see. Each pixel is actually in three parts: red, green, and blue. With these three primary additive colors all other colors can be produced. The computer rapidly sends signals to each of these pixels: turn on (and at what brightness) turn off, etc. The result is a moving picture our eyes see on the screen, like on a TV.

The retina display is unique because of the number of pixels packed per inch – four times as many as before. For example, the new iPad has a resolution of 2048x1536, with 264 pixels per inch, which means over 3.1 million pixels packed into the 9.7-inch display. Similar dense resolutions are in the iPhone 4 and the recently announced MacBook Pro Retina Display model.

When the pixels are packed so closely together, the human eye can no longer discern the individual pixels. To our eyes, reading text on a retina display is much like reading text in a book: the printing is incredibly clear.

That's what "retina display" really means: the display's ability to fool our retinas into seeing a smooth image instead of a pixelated one. It's more of a marketing term than a technical description.

If you're a photographer or you work with videos, then having a retina display on a larger screen – like the 15" MacBook Pro – makes a big difference in the details you can see. When a smaller screen is used, like on the iPhone 4, the retina display makes text visible even when the font is very small. You can zoom the image and it doesn't become blurred.

For now, Apple is the only company with retina displays, but the other companies will catch up. But by then, maybe the iPhone 6 will be out with a 3D display.

ALAN TURING

The father of computing was born 100 years ago this week

Published as "Alan Turing's impact still felt today"

June 29, 2012 (424 words)

Alan Turing is known as the father of computing. This week celebrates the centenary of his birth and the many contributions he made to the modern world.

Turing was born in England 100 years ago, on June 23, 1912. His research was so fundamental to computer science and artificial intelligence that the A.M. Turing Award, the ACM's highest honor and the equivalent of the Nobel Prize in computing, is named after him.

His early work was on the theory of computation. It led to the development of the Turing Machine, a simple tape mechanism that all computer science students must learn even today. It's a model of computation that is independent of the physical machine. The design of the Turing Machine is far removed from today's complex computers, but at the most elemental level, if a problem can't be solved with a Turing Machine, a regular computer can't solve it either. This proposition became known as the Church-Turing thesis.

Turing was also a cryptographer. He was instrumental is breaking the famous Enigma cypher that the Axis powers used during World War II. Cyber-warfare is not new: Turing's work at the Bletchley Park facility enabled the Allies to decrypt secret messages, giving the Western powers a huge advantage in early information assurance.

After the war, Turing turned his attention to artificial intelligence – the embodiment of human attributes, behaviors, and capabilities in computers. In 1950 he introduced what became known as the Turing Test, which is a test of a machine's ability to fool a human into thinking the machine is actually a real person. If the machine is indistinguishable from a knowledgeable human, using only a text-based natural language interface, then the machine has passed the Turing Test. The test ultimately leads to the question of whether or not computers can "think" – something that remains unresolved.

Turing died on June 7, 1954. For many years it was assumed he committed suicide via cyanide capsule, but recent forensic investigations have cast some doubt on this conclusion. Irrespective of the means of his demise, he was treated very poorly by the British government in the latter part of his career, and it was only in 2009 that a formal apology was made.

When one thinks of the huge technological differences that exist between the world of Turing's birth in 1912 and our world today, it's hard to believe that someone's work from so long ago (in computer terms) could still have relevance. But Turing's influence on computing was so profound that it still has impact even now.

RIP RIM

RIM has done in five years what it took Kodak 100 years to do

Published as "BlackBerry maker nearing irrelevancy"

July 6, 2012 (429 words)

When a company publically states, "there's nothing wrong with the company as it exists right now," you know there's something seriously wrong with the company. When the company's CEO also adds, "This company is not ignoring the world out there, nor is it in a death spiral," you know the company is so far out of touch with the outside world that it can't even see that it's already perceived as dead.

These amazing statements were made on a radio show this week by Thorsten Heins, chief executive of Research in Motion (RIM), the maker of the BlackBerry smartphone. Is RIM dead? Many pundits seem to think so. Personally, I think RIM still has a pulse, but it's weak and fading fast. Unless the company can turns things around very quickly, I doubt it will exist in its current form at this time next year.

In today's technology marketplace, perceptions and public opinion matter a lot. Let's examine RIM from three perspectives. The first is a business perspective. RIM has always been seen as an enterprise company, offering secure email and messaging to its corporate and government clients. But many of those customers are switching to the iPhone or Android devices. RIM's stock price has plummeted after recent announcements of record quarterly losses.

Most alarmingly, RIM announced that BB10, the next version of the operating system for the BlackBerry, has been delayed again until sometime in 2013. That's too late. Even if it's technically superior to the competition, by then it won't matter. BB10 runs the risk of becoming the OS/2 of the smartphone business.

The second perspective of RIM is from students. During the Spring

2012 semester I taught a graduate course on app development for smartphones and tablets. The students chose the platform they wanted to work on: they all picked Apple's iOS or Google's Android. Not a single student picked RIM's BlackBerry phone or PlayBook tablet. (No student picked Microsoft's Windows Phone system either.) This matters because today's students are tomorrow's decision makers, and they've already decided that RIM is irrelevant to them.

The third perspective of RIM is from the retail level. If you've ever visited an Apple store, you know they're usually packed with customers and full of energy. I recently walked past a BlackBerry store in an airport concourse. It was totally empty – not a single customer. The contrast couldn't be more striking.

Thorsten Heins may continue to read from his Monty Python script, telling anyone who will listen that RIM is "not dead yet," but in the real world, they're already gone.

SCORPIONS

They're already very nasty – do they need to glow in the dark too?

Published as "Scorpions' UV glow gives them away"

July 13, 2012 (425 words)

PHOENIX, Ariz. – Scorpions are natural technical marvels. They have a hard exoskeleton that makes then very sturdy. They can live up to four months without food or water. They can withstand the extreme temperatures of the desert. They have ferocious-looking pinchers that they use to grab their prey. And they have a vicious stinger at the tip of their curved tail, poised to strike at any time. Scorpions are the bad boys of the arachnid family. The Arizona bark scorpion makes the common Florida cockroach seem like a welcome guest.

Seeing a scorpion in your home is quite disconcerting. They can in get though openings no thicker than a credit card. They're very fast and on common beige carpet they're natural light brown color makes them almost impossible hard to spot. That is, until you step on one and they announce their presence with a burning jab to your foot.

As bad as it is to see them in your kitchen, nothing can prepare you for the sight of bright green scorpions glowing in the dark on the ground and on the walls. It's like something out of "Alien."

Most people who live in the desert have special flashlights that shine ultraviolet (UV) light, which are used to spot scorpions at night. UV flashlights are themselves examples of advanced technology sold as throwaway consumer products. They're what I call everyday magic.

When UV rays illuminate the scorpion's armor, it fluoresces. It's thought that certain proteins in their body react to the short wavelengths and reflect back the green light that our eyes can see. It's an amazing effect, rather like fireflies, but much scarier.

No one really knows for sure why scorpions glow under black light. Some scientists say it's a defense mechanism, although that assumes the scorpion's predators can see in the UV spectrum. Some say the glow is a way for the scorpion to gauge moonlight levels at night. Some think it acts as a natural sunscreen.

I wonder how our ancestors coped when they first arrived in the Wild West. I'm pretty sure they weren't carrying round UV flashlights in the days of Wyatt Earp. Maybe ignorance of the scorpion's ghostly aura helped the cowboys sleep better at night.

It also makes me wonder if we'll develop new types of radiation that cause other things to shine. The military already uses night vision goggles to see via heat signatures at night. Perhaps in the future, when someone tells you, "You've got a certain glow about you today," it will be literally true.

AIR CONDITIONING

We have Willis Carrier to thank for comfortable modern living

Published as "We can thank a cool guy for our comfort"

July 20, 2012 (431 words)

PHOENIX, Ariz. – There's a saying here in the desert: "It's a dry heat." But believe me, when it's 114°F in the shade, dry or not, it's hot. The air feels like it's coming out of a blast furnace.

According to the Weather Underground, on July 11, 2012, it was a toasty 128°F in Death Valley, Calif. That's so hot it makes a visit to Phoenix feel like a cool dip in the pool. Death Valley set a new world record for the highest low: the temperature only dropped to 107°F overnight.

Floridians are no strangers to hot weather either. The temperature might not be as high as in Arizona, but the humidity more than makes up for it. For most of the summer, it feels like you're wearing a wet blanket in a steam bath.

How did our ancestors live in such conditions? In misery, I'm guessing.

Why do we choose to live in such hot places now? Ironically, it's for the weather. But thanks to the invention of Willis Carrier, we can withstand the unpleasant months without too much discomfort and still laugh at the people up north for the rest of the year.

This week marks the 110th anniversary of the invention of air conditioning. In 1902, at the age of 25, Carrier forever changed the world. His invention was initially built for industrial application: he was trying to adjust the humidity at a printing company in Brooklyn. Now we use A/C everywhere: houses, cars, and even portable units for pets.

It's no exaggeration to say that without A/C our modern economy would not exist. We simply couldn't live and work the way we do now in hot climates without A/C to tame the environment. Indeed, modern computing centers rely on massive A/C systems to cool the machines; otherwise, their components would literally melt.

Like electricity and clean water, we take A/C for granted. But how does it work? Here in the desert, where the humidity is low, evaporative coolers are often used. These can be as large as mobile homes and are built by companies such as Tempe-based United Metal Products. They are used in large spaces like warehouses.

Everywhere else, where the humidity is higher, Carrier's creation is used. His genius was to develop a refrigeration process to pass air over cold pipes. An engineering marvel of evaporator coils and condenser coils, and the physics of converting a liquid to a gas (and back again), creates the cold air, which lowers the ambient temperature where the air blows. The result is blessed comfort – even in the summer.

HEAT SINKS

A computer with tall ears would look pretty funny

Published as "A computer with big ears? It's a cool idea"

July 27, 2012 (413 words)

PHOENIX, Ariz. – Everything here in the desert is hot. The sun is hot, the air is hot, even the pavement is hot. The constant heat means you're always thinking about how to stay cool.

Nature has it's own way of solving the heat problem. For example, the ubiquitous desert jackrabbit cools itself by radiating heat through its own network of blood vessels in its huge ears. Most other animals choose to sleep in underground burrows during the day and only come out at night, when the temperature drops.

Our modern lives run 24/7, so sleeping all day is not usually an option. And computers don't have huge ears to cool themselves, so they have to rely on technical solutions to keep them from running too hot. These solutions range from simple heat sinks to complicated liquid cooling systems.

All modern computer processors run very hot – so hot that if they were not cooled down, they'd literally melt themselves into a little puddle of metal, plastic, and silicon. The iStat Pro tool indicates that the CPU on my MacBook Pro is currently 144°F. A passive cooling system that uses heat sinks keeps the chip from getting much hotter.

Early heat sinks were made with aluminum. They have many blades that increase the surface area. The CPU is attached to the heat sink, which radiates the heat away from the chip. In many ways, these heat sinks mimic the action of the jackrabbit's ears.

When heat sinks are not enough, active cooling systems are used. We've all heard the loud noise made by fans in computers. The fans draw cooler air from the outside and blow it onto the CPU – rather like an A/C system, but without any refrigeration. Fans usually turn themselves on and off as needed, such as when the computer is doing something that requires more power. For example, when processing video files with my MacBook Pro a few days ago, the internal fans were running so loudly that I thought the notebook would levitate.

More sophisticated cooling systems are used for supercomputers with faster processors. Cold water can be piped through the innards of the computer. Refrigeration is used to cool massive data centers. Even liquid nitrogen can be used to cool components that run very hot.

Managing the heat given off by modern computers is actually one of the biggest technical challenges facing the industry. Maybe one day we'll see a more natural design to keep computers cool: big ears.

SOLAR POWER

Harnessing the sun to fuel our energy-hungry world

Published as "Sun can fuel our energy-hungry world"

August 3, 2012 (435 words)

PHOENIX, Ariz. – The Greater Phoenix area, which includes cities such as Scottsdale, Mesa, and Glendale, is collectively known as the Valley of the Sun. And for good reason: the area gets over 300 days of sunshine annually.

With the push to develop alternate sources of energy, many places in the country that enjoy abundant sunshine are investigating solar power. It's an easy way to leverage a virtually unlimited and free natural resource. You may have seen solar panel arrays dotting the landscape, sometimes covering acres of open ground. Arizona State University uses such an arrangement to power part of its ASU West campus.

Solar panels are collections of millions of tiny solar cells. As each cell is exposed to light, the energy is converted to electricity using a photovoltaic process. Most solar cells are made of silicon doped with a small impurity such as phosphorous and arsenic (N-type) or gallium and boron (P-type).

The amount of electricity produced by a single cell is very small, which is why solar panels are arranged in massive configurations. They are all lashed together to act as a power plant. And there is plenty of raw energy available. According to Peter Diamandis and Steven Kotler, authors of the book *Abundance*, "there's over 5,000 times more solar energy falling on the planet's surface than we use in a year."

Solar power is here today. It's used in numerous locations to help offset the energy needs of everything from houses to data centers. But the current reality is that solar power is rather inefficient. For example, it's affected by how much direct sunlight falls on the solar cells, which means cloudy days or dust storms (which happen fairly frequently in Phoenix) can limit their effectiveness. The current engineering techniques used to manufacture the solar cells also limits their efficiency. This is one of the reasons companies are exploring new technology and designs – but it's not an easy task. Witness the recent Solyndra bankruptcy fiasco.

Solar power shares one unfortunate characteristic with another form of alternate energy, wind power, and that's visual pollution. Just as many people view a hillside dotted with massive wind turbines to be visually unappealing, there's nothing pretty about a solar panel array. But there are innovative solutions being developed to address this problem for the solar energy sector. For example, using smart materials science to embed the solar cells into building materials such as concrete and windows, which makes for larger collectors without having the cells plastered on the roof.

As long as the sun keeps shining, our ability to harness its power will only get better.

TOE SHOES

Modern high-tech running shoes for the Ancient Greeks

Published as "Footwear tech toes the line at Olympics"

August 10, 2012 (413 words)

Some of the most popular events in London the last two weeks have involved running, such as the marathon, the 100-meter dash, and the relay race. Running captures the essence of the Olympic mottos of faster, higher, and stronger. Running is arguably the purest of sports: there is no equipment, just the human body powered by determination to go from Point A to Point B as fast as possible.

Actually, there is some equipment associated with running: the shoes. Modern footwear is a hotbed of technical innovation. With names like, "Shox Turbo," "Air Max Tailwind," and "Gel–Extreme33", these are obviously not your father's old trainers. An impressive amount of kinesiology, computer modeling and simulation of human anatomy (particularly the foot and ankle), and materials science goes into the construction of high-tech shoes like Reebok's "ZigTech Shark".

Should these sophisticated shoes be your next choice? To answer this question, I went back to the source of competitive running: the ancient Olympics of Greece.

It turns out to be a bad source. Several millennia ago, the athletes competed in the nude. There are a few "old school" competitive runners that run barefoot today. However, most modern athletes trend more towards synthetic materials and elaborate gear.

If running barefoot is too extreme for you, there are high-tech shoes that are worn without socks. They go by names like "Trail Glove." They look rather like the rubber shoes worn at the beach to avoid stepping on jellyfish and coral, but with more support.

The latest development takes these barefoot shoes to the next level.

They mimic the skeletal structure of your foot by providing separate compartments for each of your toes. They're called "Toe Shoes."

Toe shoes are marketed as a mix of technology and nature. The technology is in the engineering and manufacturing of the tight-fitting, light, and sturdy shoes. The nature is in the natural style and fit. It's the best of barefoot running but with a modern twist. Indeed, toe shoes might be the best choice for an athlete from ancient Greece if he was competing in the modern Olympics.

Personally, I think I'd find toe shoes so uncomfortable that I'd probably twist my ankle trying to run in them. For now, I'll stick with my traditional running shoes. And by "traditional" I mean old and worn out. But at least it means I've actually been using them, and isn't the ultimate goal of exercise gear to help you get some actual exercise?

Traveling with Google

Google hits the road with purchases of Zagat and Frommer's

Published as "Google hits the holiday road with recent purchases"

August 17, 2012 (394 words)

During my summer travels I used Google a lot. Searching for something has become a lot easier with location-aware applications. For example, if you're looking for the nearest bookstore, Google Maps can show you exactly where it is relative to your current location. Google Maps can then plot the optimal route for you to drive (or walk or bike) from where you are to where you want to be. If you're using Google Maps on a smartphone, the location information and travel directions are updated in real time.

If you use Google+, your search results are augmented with data taken from people in your circles. The inclusion of social network information into Google search results is somewhat controversial, but it does help when you are looking for more than just location and directions – such as when you want comments and reviews of the place you are looking for from people you trust.

Social media and customer-driven websites have changed how we make our decisions: where to eat, what to buy, where to go. Comments from your friends carry much more weight than advertisements from vendors. Google knows this very well, and to ensure that they maintain advertising revenue through their search services, they recently purchased two travel-related companies.

Last September Google acquired Zagat, a restaurant review and ratings company. Marissa Mayer (who was then Google VP, Local, Maps and Location Services, and is now the president and CEO of Yahoo!) described Zagat as, "the world's original provider of user-generated content, provides trusted and accurate restaurant ratings and curated restaurant reviews for thousands of top restaurants worldwide." Incorporating Zagat into Google search means people can make more informed choices on where to eat.

This week, Google bought Frommer's from John Wiley & Sons. Most people know Frommer's from their authoritative and comprehensive travel guides sold in bookstores and airports worldwide. Google will likely use Frommer's extensive tourism database to improve the accuracy and relevancy of their search and map capabilities.

When I think of booking travel online, I think of Expedia. Maybe one day soon I'll be thinking Google instead. After all, it's only one click from searching to purchasing, and with Google's growing portfolio of travel-related companies, it's not a stretch to conclude that they want to get into the travel business. If they do, it could be a game-changer for the travel industry.

APPLE

What is the secret to its success?

Published as "Core Apple secret? Stuff works"

August 24, 2012 (406 words)

This week Apple became the most valuable company in the world. Bigger than Microsoft. Bigger than Exxon Mobile. Bigger than Wal-Mart. On Monday, Apple's market capitalization reached $624 billion. Several analysts expect Apple to soon become the first trillion-dollar company.

What is the secret to Apple's success?

Consider Apple's latest computer operating system, OS X 10.8, known as Mountain Lion. I upgraded my aging MacBook Pro from late 2008 to this new version of the OS and it's like the computer has been given a new lease on life. Everything runs faster. Several new features, such as built-in dictation and iCloud, are great additions. But the most important thing is that, like all Apple products, it "just works."

My MacBook cost a lot of money when I first bought it. But I've been using it for almost four years now – a virtual eternity in the computer industry – and it's still a great machine. I've upgraded it several times, so that it now sports 8GB of RAM and a whopping 1TB (terabyte) of disk space.

Think of Apple's other products and the lofty place they hold in technology today. The iPhone is ubiquitous. The iPad revolutionized – nay, created – the tablet marketplace. The iPod is still going strong as a mobile music player. Apple TV is used in my house more than the regular TV.

Why do people spend thousands on a loaded MacBook Air for $3,000 when they can get a PC notebook for $300? The same reason people spend thousands on a Rolex watch when a Timex will do. Status. Elegance. Design. Beauty. Functionality.

So maybe Apple's secret to success is not a secret after all. Quite simply, it makes products and services that people love. Products they are willing to pay a premium to own. The devil, as they say, is in the details, which is why so many other companies find it so difficult to compete with them.

Apple shows little sign of slowing down. In the pipeline for this Fall are rumored to be the iPhone 5, the iPad Mini with a 7" screen, and an Apple television. Plus a deal with China Mobile that will dramatically increase the number of iPhone users in the second most populous country in the world.

Analyst Brian White of Topeka Capital Markets set a 12-month price target for Apple shares at $1,111. Who knows … eventually Apple stock may climb into Warren Buffet's Berkshire Hathaway territory.

CARDIIO

Magic app measures your pulse using the iPhone camera

Published as "Need to check your pulse? Get this app"

August 31, 2012 (410 words)

Like many people these days, I've started to track a lot of medical information related to my health. Numbers like cholesterol, blood pressure, and weight have become important. Why do they all seem to go up in sync with your age?

Ancient Greeks first measured heart pulse rate. Nowadays, the doctor or nurse usually places their fingers on your wrist, checks their watch, and scribbles a few notes on their pad. It's very low-tech, but it works.

Sadly, I've never been able to properly check my own pulse using this method. I can never find the right place to place my finger tips, I lose track of when I started counting, or I move and get an incorrect reading. I can use a blood pressure machine, which also measures your pulse, but it's not portable or convenient. So what do to?

As with all things, now there's an app for that!

I've been experimenting with a $4.99 iPhone app called Cardiio that works like a charm. The app has a very simple interface. It has a picture of a stethoscope on the screen. You touch the center of the virtual stethoscope and the app uses the iPhone's camera to analyze your face. In a few seconds it gives you a reading of your pulse rate in beats per minute (BPM).

Cardiio's technology comes out of MIT. It measures the amount of light reflected on your face, which is an indication of the amount of blood being pumped through your system. It calculates your pulse rate based on this absorption factor.

The app is not flawless. The first time I used it, it kept giving me a reading of 112 bpm, no matter what I was doing. I checked the app developer's website and it acknowledged this "rare bug" (pun intended?). It told me to re-install the app and re-boot my phone. Sigh. Some things in computing never change.

Sometimes the app has difficulty recognizing your features, but it does warn you if there are problems. Usually this is a result of poor lighting or holding the phone too close or too far from your face.

When it does work, which is most of the time, it's amazingly accurate. I did several readings at different times during the day, and compared the app's readings to the readings produced by a high-end blood pressure machine, and the app was always within 5% of the far more expensive machine's readings. It's like magic.

KINDLE FIRE

What should Amazon.com do with its tablet to be successful?

Published as "Kindle's Fire needs something new"

September 7, 2012 (423 words)

On October 25, 2011 I pre-ordered a new Kindle Fire from Amazon.com. It arrived on November 15. I returned it two weeks later. Why?

With the imminent release of a new Kindle Fire (maybe even more than one model) from Amazon.com, it may be instructive to look back and examine the reasons for my decision to return the device. I believe that the shortcomings in the initial version of the Fire need to be addressed for it to be successful in the highly competitive tablet space.

The consumer electronics marketplace is a cutthroat environment with low margins, rapid product cycles, and disruptive technologies that can make one company successful while putting others out of business virtually overnight. When Apple introduced the iPad it totally changed the tablet landscape. But tablets were not new. Microsoft had been touting them for over a decade, but they never really seemed to get it right. Apple got it right.

When other companies saw how successful the iPad was, there was a rush to get competitor tablets to market as fast as possible. Most failed. But a few gained a foothold, either by offering innovative features or a lower cost. The Kindle Fire was such a device when it debuted about a year ago.

It cost $199, which was significantly less than the iPad. It was an Android-powered tablet with a redesigned user interface. It had a 7" screen. And most importantly, it was tightly integrated with the Amazon.com experience. For example, it made shopping for products very easy. And it was touted as a great media consumption device for movies and music offered through Amazom.com's online services – particularly attractive for Amazon.com Prime customers such as myself.

But I still returned the Fire. I found the tablet too thick and heavy when compared to an iPad – and a year ago, everything was compared to an iPad. There was no 3G service – only WiFi networks were supported. It had no camera for doing video conferencing. The bookshelf metaphor was awkward to use sometimes. And it felt sluggish when using applications, probably due to an underpowered CPU and the usual issues associated with the first release of most software.

When Amazon releases the next version of the Kindle Fire, it will have to address these shortcomings. But now there is another $199 tablet it must compete with: the Nexus 7 from Google. Oh, and Apple is rumored to be releasing it's own 7" iPad very soon. In other words, Amazon.com has it's work cut out – but I hope they succeed.

GPS

Friends don't let friends drive without maps

Published as "Friends don't let friends drive with GPS"

September 14, 2012 (436 words)

There is a problem plaguing the nation: directional illiteracy. People don't know how to read maps anymore. The proliferation of GPS devices in cars has given rise to a new type of driver: one that only knows how to follow directions. Poorly.

What happens when the directions are wrong? When the GPS gives incorrect information, these people are lost – in more ways than one.

Last year I had a rental car in Los Angeles. If you've ever driven in LA you know that the freeways there are not for the faint of heart. The rental car had a GPS mounted on an improvised stand on the floor. When you start the engine the GPS starts too, and the annoying disembodied voice keeps nagging you to enter your destination until you give it some attention. The "attention" I wanted to give it was to hit the screen, but I decided to give it a try.

That was a mistake.

The interface to GPS devices are terrible – particularly the ones in rental cars. I spent way too much time sitting in the parking lot, fiddling with the wobbly arrows to enter my destination address. When you're actually driving its worse. I find GPS devices so distracting that I'm surprised they're not outlawed for in-car use like cell phones are in California.

Once I was on the highway, the GPS wouldn't shut up. Alarmingly, the directions it was giving me were plain wrong. Luckily I knew the area very well and was able to ignore the incorrect advice, but what if you placed your trust in the GPS? You'd be lost for sure – and in places like LA that's rarely a good thing.

The same thing happened to me again a few weeks later in Toronto. The GPS was telling me to take a turn off the highway to get to downtown, but I knew that the suggested route would take me into Lake Ontario instead.

I have a friend that relies on GPS in the car all the time. But the GPS is old and hasn't been updated in a long time, because the cables and software needed to do so are no longer available. So the GPS gives directions based on road conditions from 7 years ago; no wonder it's wrong so much of the time.

A recent Dilbert cartoon showed Alice screaming at a GPS because it was giving wrong directions. I know the feeling. But arguing with machines is a losing proposition.

For cities that I'm not familiar with, I always study a map. It's a low-tech but effective backup for GPS devices that fail.

DO NOT DISTURB

Apple's iOS 6 brings Sandman to the digital age

Published as "iOS 6 allows us to sleep with no worries"

September 21, 2012 (432 words)

At 6:10am on Wednesday morning I was woken by a loud text message alert informing me that Endeavour was a "go" for an early morning departure for California from KSC. Another loud message alert arrived at 7:23am telling me that the 747 was "wheels-up" and the shuttle was starting its long journey to Los Angeles. A few weeks ago it was a 4:09am notice that an Atlas V rocket had blasted off with NASA's radiation belt probes.

Now, I'm a space junky, which is why I subscribe to these sorts of notices. But it sure would be nice to turn them off occasionally. Night launches are great fun to watch, but sometimes sleep takes priority.

The simplest solution is to turn off the phone's ringer – put it in "silent" mode. This makes the text alert problem go away, but it also means you never hear the phone ring, even in case of emergencies. We've all experienced the dreaded 3:00am call from family or friends in some far-away place with important news.

Hotels solved this problem long ago. Like many non-technical solutions, it's simple yet effective. You put a "Do Not Disturb" sign on the door and the maid knows not to come bursting in to change the bed at 7:00am. You can also call the front desk and tell them to hold all calls, which they will do – unless it's an emergency. The same for the door sign: hotel management can still get in if there's a real need to do so.

On September 19, Apple released iOS 6, a free upgrade to the iPhone operating system. Among its many new capabilities is a "Do Not Disturb" feature that does the equivalent of hanging a door sign <u>and</u> calling the front desk. It can be turned on manually or scheduled for recurring times, such as at night. When it's on, a little moon icon is shown at the top of the phone.

The "Do Not Disturb" feature lets you silence all incoming calls, text alerts, and push messages. However, you can tell it to let people on your Favorites list or special contacts get through, which means those emergency calls from people you know would still reach you. It even has a special setting to let calls through if it's a second call from the same number within three minutes – a typical emergency scenario when someone is calling from a pay booth or a borrowed cell phone.

Why did it take so long for a technical solution to arrive for my so-called smartphone? Well, better late than never I suppose. Welcome iSandman.

SAM THE RECORD MAN

Technology changes how we experience music

Published as "Technology changes how we rock out"

September 28, 2012 (425 words)

I bought my first CD in 1988. It was called "Show Me" from the Canadian band 54•40. I can still vividly recall purchasing the CD because it was a freezing cold January night in Toronto, and I had to walk a long way to buy the disc from the Sam the Record Man store on Yonge St.

Sam Sniderman, who founded the iconic music store (it held the same status in Canada as Tower Records did in California), died this week at the age of 92. His passing gave me pause to think about how technology changes how we experience music.

In 1977 I bought my first cassette tape, "Hotel California" by The Eagles. I listened to it on a portable player in the back of my parents' car on a holiday road trip. Music on a cassette limits you to sequential playback. You listen to the tracks in a fixed order, and it's hard to skip to the next song – all you can choose is the side. A tape forces you to enjoy the music as the artist intended.

In 1979 I bought my first vinyl record, a used copy of "Three Hearts" by Bob Welch. I bought the album at a store called Cheap Thrills in Montréal – a store that I would eventually spend many hours (and many dollars) in over the years. Music on a record is more visceral. Your hands touch the sleeves as you flip through the record bins. You can almost feel the needle cut into the grooves. You can hear the imperfections, the scratches, the hisses and pops. But you can also play any track you want, in any order, with the limits of one side at a time and no repeating tracks automatically. I sold my entire record collection in 1998.

In 1999 I downloaded my first MP3 song, "Let Forever Be" by the Chemical Brothers. Like most music at that time, the file probably came from Napster. I played my limited MP3 collection on a Diamond Rio – a precursor to the iPod. But I could play any track, in any order, and create my own playlist – it was liberating. After Napster closed my digital music came mostly from iTunes and Amazon.com.

Since 2009 I stream most of my music using services like Pandora and Spotify. I don't bother to download it anymore. Algorithms recommend songs similar to the ones I like. But a disembodied computer can never replace the love of music or the feeling of camaraderie that someone like Sam shared with his customers.

DOCUMENT IDENTIFIERS

Why do geeks keep inventing new ways to confuse us?

Published as "It's time to put old search methods on bookshelf where they belong"

October 5, 2012 (464 words)

What does QA76.6 mean to you?

To most people, this odd string means nothing. But if you're a computer science bookworm, and if you're old enough to have been in an actual bricks-and-mortar library, you might remember that this is the call number for computer books. QA76.6 is an example of the Library of Congress subject classification system, created in 1897 to help libraries catalog their books. Other systems are also used, such as the Dewey Decimal Classification (DDC) system, invented in 1876. Both systems were designed to help the library, not necessarily the user.

For example, if you have the QA76.6 call number, you know which stack of shelves to look at to find your book. But the call number is more like a neighborhood name than a specific street address, so you still have to scan the shelves yourself, manually looking for the book, hoping that someone else didn't misplace the book on the wrong shelf.

There's a good reason that Barnes & Noble doesn't use these systems to catalog the books in their stores: no one would understand it. People think in terms of words, topics, and ideas – not numbers. That's why computer books are shelved under descriptors like "Computers" and not QA76.6.

So why do libraries use it? Probably for the same reason publishers still uses other numbers to tracks things like magazines (ISSN) and books (ISBN-10 and ISBN-13): it's a reasonable way for them to manage their internal catalog. But it's a horrible way for a user to find anything. For readers, books have words, not numbers.

Of course, if you're like most students today, the whole concept of physically browsing the stacks in a real library – or even a real bookstore – is terribly antediluvian. You don't need to remember weird strings like QA76.6 or 005 to find computer books. You use Google. All you need are a few search strings and you're off – browsing the virtual stacks (the "hits" page returned by Google).

Modern libraries and bookstores are increasingly online. So you might think that they'd avoid the mistakes of the past and use a better, more understandable, human-friendly system to identify their documents. You'd be wrong.

The latest development is the Digital Object Identifier (DOI). It's yet another way to refer to a book using a number instead of its title. The word "digital" refers to the document in electronic format (e.g., a PDF file), but since we're analog, not digital, it tells you where the geeks' priorities are.

My recent book has a DOI of 10.1007/978-3-642-32122-1. When I entered this gibberish into Google, it assumed it was an equation! It displayed a calculator and gave me the result -32767.9896721. Maybe sales are down. Sigh.

And don't get me started on URLs, IP addresses, and domain names.

CALL TREES

Your call is not very important to us...

Published as "Press 1 for frustration, 2 to give up"

October 12, 2012 (425 words)

Every time I get stuck in a labyrinthine call tree I think of the Dilbert cartoon where Dogbert amuses himself by working on the "Customer Disservice" line. Dogbert's opening question to the customer calling is, "How may I abuse you?"

It's funny because it's so close to the truth. Except that Dogbert is a person (well, a comical dog), whereas I typically am speaking with the disembodied voice of a computer. The voice is fake, but the abuse and frustration is very real.

A "call tree" is slang for an automated help system that many companies use. Ironically, it's neither automated nor helpful. If the system were automated, it wouldn't force all the effort back to the customer. How many times have you entered account information using the phone's awkward keypad, only to be transferred to another system (or even a person) that immediately asked you for the same information? That's not automation, that's duplication.

As for being helpful, the system makes more sense when you remember that "help" doesn't refer to helping you, the customer. It refers to helping the company to reduce costs by using a computer system that appears to be purposely designed to be so complicated that most customers give up in frustration and hang up. Problem solved.

Hitting '0' (zero) repeatedly, no matter what the system is asking you, sometimes works to get a real, live account representative online. But the last time I tried this, the system informed me that I had a problem with my account (Duh! That's why I was calling!), and then transferred me to a representative. Then the call was cutoff. Twice.

I find it particularly galling when the automated system is given human-like characteristics. For example, the fake sound of someone typing information on a loud keyboard is meant to sooth the user with familiar actions. "The system must be doing something for me, I can hear it typing away." Such anthropomorphosis is a pathetic attempt to mask the inanity of the situation.

Many companies use automated call systems in the misguided belief that it will save them money, but I doubt it saves them anything – other than repeat customer business. These systems are complicated to engineer and expensive to install. They rarely work as expected. I am skeptical that their cost saving are more than the cost needed to just hire a real person – and a local person, not somewhere in India – to be a proper customer service agent.

Technology is good for automating many things. Customer service is not one of them.

NOBEL PRIZE IN PHYSICS

Fundamental physics research may lead to quantum computers

Published as "Quantum physics at heart of computer"

October 19, 2012 (439 words)

The 2012 Nobel Prize in Physics to Serge Haroche (Collège de France and Ecole Normale Supérieure in Paris) and David Wineland (National Institute of Standards and Technology in Boulder) for their work in "measuring and manipulating individual particles while preserving their quantum-mechanical nature."

In English, this means they found different but equally interesting ways to work with quantum particles. A quantum particle is one that has the seemingly paradoxical property of being on ("there") and off ("not there") at the same time. Nearly 80 years ago the Austrian physicist Erwin Schrödinger proposed a famous thought experiment, wherein a cat is placed in a closed box. Inside the box the cat is simultaneously alive and dead. We only know the truth when we open the box, when the cat instantaneously becomes alive or dead. In our normal world it's obviously impossible to be in both states at the same time. But in the weird world of quantum physics it's reality.

In physics, being in two states at once is known as superposition. When the particles collapse into one of two choices, the act is known as decoherence. Quantum particles exhibit this behavior of duality, but the very act of viewing or measuring the particles causes them to collapse into one of the two states. The Nobel Prize was awarded to the two scientists for innovative ways of trapping and studying individual quantum particles without them collapsing into discrete states.

This is all very heady Star Trek stuff, but what does it have to do with technology today?

Today, not too much. But tomorrow, possibly everything.

Quantum physics is at the heart of a new type of fantastic machine known as a "quantum computer". It's in the early experimental stages now, but when it becomes a reality it could change the very nature of computing.

In today's computers, all operations are based on digital logic. A single bit is either on (1) or off (0). Everything we do with computers is founded on this simple principle. Representing images, running programs, doing Google searches, all use this binary system.

In a quantum computer, bits become "qubits" (quantum bits). They can be on (1) or off (0) at the same time. This means certain problems can be solved exponentially faster than a regular computer. Problems like cryptography, which are at the heart of secret communications and credit card transactions, are currently "unbreakable" but become solvable in real time.

Quantum computing represents the biggest change in computing since the introduction of vacuum tubes. It would be that big. Now we just need to get the engineers involved to turn science fiction into science fact.

WINDOWS 95

Start me up

Published as "Newest Windows release seems like old times"

October 26, 2012 (414 words)

The latest and greatest version of Windows is about to hit the shelves. It promises the fundamentally change how most people use their computers. Microsoft has "bet the company" on this new release of Windows, so there's a lot riding on its success.

The new OS has a totally revamped user interface. There's a new way to start programs. Networking and sharing files promises to be a lot easier than it is now. A new web browser gets you online in no time, and it's supposed to be a lot faster than the competition.

To use this version of Windows, you'll probably want to get a new computer. Although it can run on many existing PCs, you'll only experience the full benefits of the OS's new capabilities with newer hardware.

* * *

Everything I wrote above is true. But it was for Windows 95, which was released August 24, 1995 – over 17 years ago. It was the last truly revolutionary release of Windows before today's release of Windows 8. The change from Windows 3.1 to Windows 95 was as striking as the change from Windows 7 (or XP) to Windows 8.

In 1995, the local Egghead computer store was open from 12:00am – 2:00am to celebrate the release of the new operating system. People were lined up outside long before midnight, waiting to get the software. Now people line up for the latest iPhone.

I waited one month before I installed Windows 95. One reason for the delay is that I had to get a new computer first – the old one had just 2MB of RAM and could not be upgraded. Even with my new computer I had to buy an additional 8MB of RAM ($389 from Egghead) for Windows to work properly. By comparison, my current MacBook Pro has 8GB of RAM – an amazing 500x increase.

I also purchased the "Microsoft Plus" CD, which had a few tools, some games, and sample videos. The song "Good Times" by Edie Brickell became the sound of the late summer of 1995 for many people. Just seeing videos play smoothly on your PC was a memorable event at the time. Weezer's "Buddy Holly" was also in the sample video folder. It was quite sophisticated too: it inserted the band playing live into the 1950's setting of "Happy Days".

Just as Egghead is gone, I think the time for getting excited over a new OS is past. As the owner of Al's Diner would sigh, "Yeah. Yeah-yeah-yeah..."

JAVA

The language that began with promise has become a disaster

Published as "Java's promise becomes a disaster"

November 2, 2012 (409 words)

I'm writing this on Halloween, when scary things happen. The programming language Java, which started life with such promise in 1995, has mutated into a computer monster. Like Frankenstein's creation, it needs to be killed to spare us any more misery.

Like many people, my father uses his computer to play games online. In particular, card games like bridge from Yahoo!. These games require Java to be running in the web browser. A recent update of Java had caused many of Yahoo!'s games to stop working. But of course I didn't know this at first; when programs stop working on a Windows computer it could be due to any number of reasons – only laborious detective work can determine the root cause.

Java was originally developed as a new programming language by Sun Microsystems for web applications. The idea was to write one program in a single language and have that program run on all platforms (Windows, Mac, Linux). The motto was, "write once, run anywhere." In practice, this soon became, "write once, debug everywhere."

The Java program has its own auto-update mechanism that seems to have a mind of its own. Like a zombie it can't be killed; it keeps running even when I turned it off. I eventually found that the current version of Java on the computer was Version 6 Update 37. Yes, 37. What kind of defective program needs 37 updates and still doesn't work? The answer is a program so full of security vulnerabilities that it's being patched constantly. Can you imagine if this was a car, with 37 recalls for the same model year?

In fact, the situation was worse than that. There were three other versions of Java installed on the computer, all quietly working against each

87

other with malevolent intent. It seemed their main job was to ensure no program worked properly, other than the window that kept popping up with the message, "Please wait."

I eventually managed to uninstall all versions of Java. Then I did a fresh install of the latest version, which is Version 7 Update 9. Really? 9 updates already? This is not software engineering. It's hacking of the worse order. Oracle, which now owns Java through their acquisition of Sun in 2010, should be ashamed.

The Yahoo! games are working again on my dad's computer. But I feel like I've been party to spreading a disease to bring them back to life. Java needs to be eradicated.

VOTING

It will be new technology versus aging voters in future elections

Published as "Digital democracy on the way? Don't count on it"

November 9, 2012 (405 words)

I've read a lot of predictions of how we'll vote in future elections. Paper ballots will disappear. Everything will be online. We'll use our smartphones. We'll "like" the presidential candidate we want to elect using Facebook.

It's not going to happen.

At least, it won't happen for a long time, and it probably won't happen in the way people think. New technology rarely supplants existing technology. Instead, it co-exists for many years.

There are many problems associated with how we vote today. Renting buildings, hiring workers at all the polling stations, driving to the correct precinct and lining up to mark your ballot are all time-consuming and expensive undertakings. Voter intimidation is still prevalent. The papers forms are long and confusing to use. No one really can digest the lengthy amendments while standing behind curtain with pen in hand. And we all remember the problems with hanging chads from the federal election in 2004.

But for all its flaws, the current voting system mostly works. It's low-tech in most locations, which means it's unlikely to fail. There are multiple redundancies in place to verify that the process is followed properly. And there are always real people, actual live humans, available to help when a problem arises. No frustrating automated help systems.

In contrast, electronic voting machines today are fraught with flaws. Like all computers, they are prone to breaking down at the least opportune moment – like on election day in a remote location where no one can fix it. They are known to have security vulnerabilities, which makes voter fraud easier for those with a little technical savvy. And no matter what the engineers promise, the machines will always be more complicated to use than a paper ballot.

Over time, the technology will improve. But the demographics are against electronic voting for the foreseeable future. The aging population of baby boomers means there will actually be an increased propensity to keep things simple. One might think that younger voters (the iPhone generation) would drive the changes, and eventually they will, but for now the seniors will decide.

The most likely scenario is a gradual increase in digital democracy. The old voting system will slowly fade away, but like the post office it will always have a role for some segment of the population. The overall system becomes more complex, but for individuals it will become easier – as long as you like dealing with more choices.

HYBRID SHOPPING

Order online and pickup in-store doesn't always work

Published as "'Hybrid' shopping is easy ... in theory"

November 16, 2012 (421 words)

Brick-and-mortar stores continue to see their sales decline due to giant online retailers like Amazon.com. There has been an increase in "show rooming," where shoppers browse the aisles at "real" local stores, compare prices using apps on their smartphones specially designed for that purpose, and then order the item they are looking at from an online competitor for less cost.

One way big box stores have tried to combat show rooming is called hybrid shopping. The customer browses the store's website from home, orders the product they want, and picks it up from the store in person later that day. The idea is that you get the lower online price but you don't have to wait for (or pay for) delivery; you get what you ordered almost right away. You also get to avoid the long lines at the checkout, since the store has a special area set aside for in-store pickup for pre-paid hybrid shoppers.

That's the theory. In my experience, it doesn't always work in practice.

About a month ago I was anxiously waiting for the new version of a product to be released. The first version had good reviews, but the second version promised numerous improvements. It was available for pre-order online, but it was also available for hybrid shopping with immediate availability from a major chain. Even though it would cost me more, I chose to order it from the store's website and arrange for pickup later in the day.

When I got to the store, the special pickup area wasn't so special. It was the same desk where returns were handled, and there were long lines. When I eventually spoke to a salesperson, they had no idea what I was talking about; hybrid shopping was apparently news to them. No one even knew where in the store the new product was kept. A few intercom announcements later, a manager came over and eventually the product I had ordered was located, hidden away in a locker that no one had the keys to.

When I got home and opened the box it was the wrong product; it was the old version, not the new one. I returned to the store and tried to sort things out. The store staff were courteous but clueless. I asked for a refund and went home. I ordered it online from a competitor. It cost less. There was no sales tax. It arrived in a few days. And it was the right version. Lesson learned. And for the store, another lost sale.

THANKSGIVING

Technology today can help make you healthy, wealthy, and wise

Published as "Giving thanks for technology that improves our lives"

November 23, 2012 (434 words)

Thanksgiving is traditionally a time for us to take a step back and give thanks for all the good things in our lives. It's also an appropriate time to reflect on the many modern conveniences that improve the quality of our lives. To paraphrase an old proverb, technology today can help make you healthy, wealthy, and wise.

Healthy: Sophisticated drugs and specialized bio-medical devices have had a dramatic impact on our health and longevity. Common prescriptions like cholesterol-lowering statins and blood pressure medication have reduced the risk of heart diseases for millions of people. Mechanical hips and knee replacements keep people mobile who otherwise might be house bound.

The insulin pump I uses is a great example of a life-changing technology. Without it, I'd be stuck (pardon the pun) with multiple daily injections with a syringe. Using the pump has made me healthier by better maintenance of my blood glucose levels.

Wealthy: In one of my favorite novels, Somerset Maugham's "The Razor's Edge," the main character Larry Darrell comes to realize the time-honored lesson that wealth isn't measured solely in terms of how much money you have. A better measure of true wealth comes from your relationships with friends and family.

In Larry's time (circa World War I), most people lived close to their friends and family. Frequent travel to far-away places was limited to a small segment of society. These days, we're scattered across the country and around the globe. Many professionals are road warriors. Distance and absence can make maintaining healthy relationships much harder. Fortunately, technology can help.

We take cell phones for granted now, but they are marvelous inventions that let us speak to people without being tethered to home. Dick Tracy's fantastic wrist radio from the 1940s has become a reality. It's so commonplace we don't even think about how magical it really is.

Smartphones and applications like Apple's FaceTime and Microsoft's Skype have made communication even better. Now we can have video conversations, share photos, and really "be there" – no matter where "there" is. As with the classic AT&T advertisement from the 1980s, we can "reach out and touch someone" without thinking too much about where we are or where they are.

Wise: The Internet and search engines have put the world's knowledge at our fingertips. The ability to immediately find answers online to almost any question is something our ancestors could only dream of. Technology has made it possible for us to have the appearance of wisdom.

Of course, wisdom is the judicious use of knowledge – and that can't be replaced by technology. And for that I'm thankful.

GANGNAM STYLE

YouTube and social networks are disrupting big media

Published as "YouTube killed the video start? Possibly"

November 30, 2012 (390 words)

The latest pop sensation is a rapper who goes by the name of PSY. Last week his hit, "Gangnam Style," became the most viewed video ever on YouTube. He even bumped Justin Bieber off his throne.

As I write this, "Gangnam Style" has been seen over 840 million times. It may soon become the first video with one billion viewings. In comparison, top-rated network shows like "The Voice" and "The X Factor" peak at about 10 million viewers.

The guy is singing almost entirely in Korean – a language most people can't understand. The song is about living large in Gangnam – a small but wealthy district of Seoul that most people have never heard of. The video is shown online only – not on TV.

So how did "Gangnam Style" become so popular? In a word, disintermediation.

Word spread about the video through social networks. "Gangnam Style" has over 5.5 million Facebook "likes". The video can be seen at any time, for no cost, on Google's YouTube service.

From a global perspective, there was very little in the way of traditional marketing for "Gangnam Style" – it made PSY famous without the help of traditional "big media" companies. Since he became famous online, he's parlayed that popularity into the regular media too.

YouTube and social networks are disruptive technologies that are dramatically changing how we experience entertainment. The artist can connect directly with the audience without going through conventional distribution channels. There is comparatively little cost and potentially huge rewards. There is always the danger of getting lost in the crowd, but if something has legs it will run to the top of the charts all by itself – pushed there if needed by a global fan base who use their mobile smartphones more than their family's television to watch shows.

I think PSY is also popular because he doesn't look much like a Hollywood "product." He's 35, not 18. He dances quite well, but looking at him you wouldn't think he could dance at all. He dresses like a metrosexual geek. Perhaps people think, "If he can do it, so can I." It's empowering.

Most of the "Gangnam Style" video is without meaning – just escapist nonsense presented in a humorous and self-effacing manner. Who knew that riding an invisible pony around would be so much fun? Not that there's anything wrong with that.

CAR SOFTWARE

How long before you have to sync your car with iTunes?

Published as "Software turns cars into PCs on wheels"

December 7, 2012 (401 words)

Consider the following scenario. You're driving down the highway and reach to turn on the radio. Instead of hearing music, you see a cryptic text message appear on the radio's display indicating that a software update is in progress. Please wait…

Now imagine the same thing happening to other parts of your car. You try to shift intro reverse while parking and the transmission control system says it needs a software update. You adjust the air conditioner and the temperature computer says it needs a software update.

If each of these computer control systems was an app, they'd be updating themselves constantly.

Does this sound far fetched? It's not. Today's cars are marvels of modern engineering, but they are also fast becoming complex computers on wheels. And we all know how dependable computer software is.

The recent update pushed out by Ford Motor Company for their MyFordTouch infotainment system is just one example of how software now controls many aspects of present-day driving. The Ford update is applied by downloading the patch from their website, copying the file to a USB key, and inserting the key into the car's USB slot on the dashboard.

What would happen if a virus got into the car's computer systems? I for one don't relish the idea of driving around in a hacked car, wondering when it will be turned into a mobile member of a botnet.

Every time computers are added to electro-mechanical systems, a tradeoff is made between added functionality and decreased reliability. Luxury carmakers lead the way with new gizmos that add to manufacturing costs and user frustration with questionable tangible benefits. For example, when BMW introduced the Microsoft Windows CE-powered iDrive joystick control in their top-of-the-line 7-Series cars in 2001 there was a consumer backlash regarding the system's confusing interface.

I've been fortunate to work on several funded projects from car companies like BMW. I've seen how the "ultimate driving machine" has morphed into a very complex embedded system that goes very fast. In many cases, the development cost of the software has outstripped the cost of the hardware in the car.

At some point we as consumers will have to push back against the increasingly complicated controls. I don't want the dashboard to resemble a pilot's cockpit. I just want to turn the key and go. I don't need rotating mirrors and voice recognition systems to help me do that.

APOLLO 17

It's time to re-ignite the fire of manned space missions

Published as "Will we ever see a marvel to equal the spectacle of Apollo landings?"

December 14, 2012 (424 words)

Last week marked the 40th anniversary of Apollo 17. It was the final manned mission to the moon. It launched on Dec. 7, 1972. It was the only nighttime launch of the Apollo program. I've seen numerous space shuttles and rocket launches at night, but I can only imagine what it must have been like to see the massive Saturn V rocket blast off, it's five huge F1 engines burning brightly against the dark sky.

The 3-person crew of Apollo 17 returned safely to Earth on Dec. 19. Subsequent Apollo moon missions were planned, but they never took place. We haven't put our feet on the moon since then.

The Apollo program was a technical marvel. It was also a political statement aimed primarily at the Soviet Union. And it was a social phenomenon that brought together our nation like few other events have done.

This week the secretive X-37B mini-shuttle launched into orbit aboard an Atlas V rocket. It's the third launch of this Air Force program in three years and the second for this particular vehicle. It too is technically interesting, but the differences between the X-37B program and the Apollo program couldn't be more pronounced.

Apollo was a public effort. It was grand in aspiration and huge in scale. The Saturn V rocket stood 363 feet high and was 33 feet wide. By comparison, the X-37B mission is classified; no one really knows what it's for or what its capabilities are. In many ways it acknowledges the militarization of space. And at 29 feet long it's a small vehicle – barely more than a drone.

We rely on foreign countries to ferry our astronauts to the space station. Our next heavy-lift rockets are years away from trials. The next country likely to put a man on the moon is China.

How can we get the sprit of Apollo back? Maybe by picking up where Apollo left of, with voyages of exciting scientific discovery. It's hard to get kids interested in remote-controlled ships clouded in secrecy (whatever their intrinsic value). But kids do get engaged when they see exciting research being done – research they can aspire to be part of.

It's particularly ironic that the Apollo program was canceled just as the real science was starting. Astronaut Harrison Schmitt, who walked on the lunar surface as part of Apollo 17, was a geologist. The BBC dubbed him, "the last man and first scientist" on the moon. It feels like we had just got started when we stopped. When will we get started again?

12-21-12

It may be the end of the world as we know it but I feel fine

Published as "Mayan calendar didn't foretell doom"

December 21, 2012 (413 words)

If you're reading this column, then I guess we survived the Mayan apocalypse. I have no way of knowing how really things turned out, since I'm writing this before December 21, 2012 – the prophesied Day of Doom. However, I'm an optimist at heart, so I prefer to think that 12-21-12 was just a big misunderstanding.

The Mayan's had a complicated way of tracking time. They used multiple calendars that were cyclic in nature – which is at the heart of the confusion regarding their "prediction" that the world would end. As far as we know, they never said any such thing.

Imagine you were living nearly a thousand years ago. Your technology was extremely rudimentary, but you were intelligent and inquisitive. How would you track the hours in a day, the days in a month, or the length of a year? The notion of a "day" was limited to sunup to sundown. Even the concept of a "month" hadn't been invented.

Given such limitations, the Mayans created a complex calendar system that was part religious and part celestial. They were able to measure the passage of time with impressive accuracy. Sadly, they were unable to use it to predict their own unfortunate demise.

This month was numerologically interesting for another reason: we witnessed the last of the three-digit day-month-year combinations. December 12, 2012 can be written as 12-12-12. This is similar to last year's 11-11-11, and the previous year's 10-10-10. These rare days won't occur again until the 22nd century, on January 1, 2101: 1-1-1.

2012 was also a leap year. As I wrote here in March, calculating leap years is not easy. Nature doesn't always follow our clean calculations. Leap years are another reason early calendar systems were occasionally adjusted by adding additional holidays as needed.

Many civilizations have predicted the end of days. The Mayan's foretelling of 12-21-12 is just the latest in the series. I think people read too much into these things; just because the battery in my watch died doesn't mean time is ending – it just means I need to get a new battery.

The Mayan's prediction notwithstanding, I don't plan on moving to a mountain retreat in Montana now any more than I did so for the Year 2000 "calamity" that never happened. That said, sometimes it's better to be safe than sorry. This week I'm making a pilgrimage to Mexico where ancient Mayan temples still exist; maybe I'll stop by with a modest donation – just in case.

LOOKING BACK AT 2012

Mobile, cloud, and social computing were big in 2012

Published as "What was hot, what was not in technology in 2012"

December 28, 2012 (431 words)

At the start of 2012 I predicted that, "the very nature of what we call 'computing' will continue to change. These changes have already begun, but will gain momentum at the edge (mobile computing), in the center (cloud computing), and on the connections (social computing) of our technical infrastructure." As the year draws to a close let's take a look back and see if these predictions were accurate.

Mobile Computing: Smartphones and tablets enjoyed a tremendous year in 2012. Apple's new iPhone 5 broke sales records. Google's Android continued to make inroads, but with some confusion related to different hardware platforms and software versions. The app ecosystem blossomed into a multi-billion dollar marketplace. Smartphone apps have become so powerful that sales of stand-alone products like digital cameras and GPS devices have plummeted.

Tablets were big news in 2012. Apple's iPad Mini – a product that Steve Jobs said would never be made – was extremely popular. Amazon.com's Kindle Fire HD was well received. Many manufacturers are offering hybrid tablet/notebook systems running Microsoft's new Windows 8 operating system. Personally I think these hybrid systems are the worst of both worlds, and the mixed-mode user interface of Windows 8 will be seen in the future as a misstep on the road to a tablet-focused computing environment.

Cloud Computing: The one question I was asked more than any other in 2012 was, "What is cloud computing?" The phrase has gone mainstream, but the concept remains fuzzy. As cloud computing matures in the coming years, unless you work in IT you won't know (or care) how it works.

Of great interest to me is how startup companies are using the cloud to compete with the bigger companies at very low cost. The cloud is letting these small companies grow very fast, to support millions of users, without the capital investment that would have been needed just a few years ago.

Social Computing: By far the biggest news story of 2012 driven by social computing was Psy's "Gangnam Style" video that went viral through YouTube. The video has now passed one billion views. They say imitation is the sincerest form of flattery; there are hundreds of very funny parodies of the South Korean's video online.

The social networking giant Facebook went public in 2012. Their IPO was commonly seen as a business disaster brought down in part by technical failings of the computerized stock trading system. Their initial price was $38, but the shares quickly dropped to half that value. Insiders trading on the pre-IPO private markets made money, but the public got soaked. Some things never change.

ABOUT THE AUTHOR

Scott Tilley is a Professor in the Department of Education and Interdisciplinary Studies at the Florida Institute of Technology, where he is Director of Computing Education. He is Chair of the Steering Committee for the IEEE Web Systems Evolution (WSE) series of events and a Past Chair of the ACM's Special Interest Group on Design of Communication (SIGDOC). He is an ACM Distinguished  Lecturer. His current research focuses on software testing, cloud computing, educational technology, STEM outreach, and system migration. He writes the weekly "Technology Today" column for the *Florida Today* newspaper (Gannett). His most recent book is *Testing iOS Apps with HadoopUnit: Rapid Distributed GUI Testing* (Morgan & Claypool, 2014).

www.ingramcontent.com/pod-product-compliance
Lightning Source LLC
Chambersburg PA
CBHW071227050326
40689CB00011B/2488